AMIN ⸻

# GIVE
## FIRST

# TAKE
## LAST

A Path to Learning Perseverance,
Building Resilience, and
Impacting Your Community

Entrepreneurship is a long process. We as people think that the process comes naturally and that the person never fails. However, as we know that is not the case. Amin is the epitome of the American Dream and has lived what I believe is the long process to Entrepreneurship. Through this process, he has had to overcome tragedies, obstacles, while also dealing with his own personal health issues. But through it all he has become the American Dream. He has taken his success and has given what he has learned back to his community. He mentors young professionals trying to make it in today's world, helps lift others up in need, and gives back to his community in many, many other ways. This entrepreneurship journey has made him the man he is today.

**—Craig Morgan, Mayor Round Rock, Texas**

Amin, your book has changed the way I think. I have always been a believer in life's purpose but was always confused by what my purpose is. After reading your book, I have started to ponder upon my life and its purpose. It has made me realize that there is a reason why I was born on this earth and that God has a plan for me.

**— Abdul Samad, Business Owner**

I'm so happy to recommend this book authored by my friend, Amin Salahuddin. It is one of the best books on serving communities of color I have ever read. It is thought provoking, amazingly insightful, and downright inspiring. Amin is not afraid to share his life story of facing pain and sacrifice, while overcoming racism and displaying resiliency. These experiences have shaped him into becoming the leader that he is. He shares novel ideas, suggestions, and tips to help build community-based infrastructures that have been largely ignored. Amin's technology - based healthcare non-profit which focuses on providing healthcare to the uninsured, will revolutionize healthcare access for both insured and uninsured.

**—Jill C. Ramirez, Co-founder, Latino Healthcare Forum**

Amin Salahuddin has written a must-read for anyone considering philanthropy or entrepreneurship. This collection of personal stories reminds us about the importance of and the impression we make by giving back, along with the value we create when we invest in local communities while following our principles. This is an inspirational must-read!

**— Cristal Finke, MPH**

Inspiring story from an inspiring man. What a journey! I had no idea. I really did love the book and felt its honesty. I will share it with friends and family.

**—Susan Harris, Registered Nurse and Neighbor**

I've been searching for peace in my life and haven't been accomplishing many of my projects and goals. In *Give First, Take Last*, Amin describes the times he had faced death and experienced financial losses as he chased his dream of becoming an entrepreneur. He shares his life lessons and focuses on what's important in life, including how to have a positive mindset through life's challenges. If he can accomplish all I know he's done with the past emotional traumas he's endured, then I can surely meet my goals and live a life centered in peace! Thank you for sharing your wisdom with us and reminding us of what gets in the way of achieving our dreams.

**— Cathy Smith, Neighbor**

This book contains practical experiences we all can learn from. I'd say, it definitely holds a lot of treasures that are already dug up, polished, and showcased in an eloquent display by Amin! Well done!

**— Sam Sheikh, Community Leader**

When I first met Amin, I never would have imagined how powerful someone's beliefs could be despite failures. Amin never gave up. He kept rising again and again until he reached his goal. This book certainly brings a life-changing experience for so many people by the realities of life. Amin's mantra of giving first and taking last is not only a gift but uplifts the soul.

— Manish Tripathi, Business Owner

I have learned things in this book that I never thought I would ever know. It is like a journey of self-discovery. The book is full of amazing stories and breathtaking experiences. It reminds me of the saying "What doesn't kill you makes you stronger." It is true that life is a journey full of struggles. In this book I have learned different ways of looking at calamities of life. Thank you, Amin, I am forever grateful.

— Hayat Shaban, Realtor

Amin, I just finished your book and I wanted to say thank you. I was inspired by it and have started to think about my life in a new way.

— Dipak Patel, Neighbor

*Give First, Take Last* is a very enlightening and in-spiring book of the life journey of Amin Salahud-din which reflects the true personality and nature of Amin giving first. I can testify that Amin is a friend, a mentor, and an inspiration for me as well. This book tells us about the events, circumstances and the emotional setbacks that inspired and led Amin to go into the medical field and start a nonprofit clinic that is serving thousands of patients. I am one of these patients who has personally experienced the benefits from his legacy.

— Rizwan Shuja, Author and Motivational Speaker

Publication date: April 2023

ISBN Softcover Print: 979-8-9880307-0-6
ISBN Hardcover Print: 979-8-9880307-1-3
ISBN eBook: 979-8-9880307-2-0

Library of Congress Control Number: 023905210

This publication is designed to provide accurate and authoritative information regarding the subject matter covered. It is sold with the understanding that the author or the publisher is not engaged in rendering any type of legal or professional information. If expert assistance is required, the services of a competent professional should be sought.

1. Giving 2. Leadership 3. Success 4. Community 5. Business 6. Clinics 7. Legacy 8. Mentorship

I Salahuddin, Amin. II Give First Take Last

*Give First Take Last* may be purchased at special quantity discounts for sales promotions, fundraising, book clubs, or educational purposes for nonprofits, schools, and universities as well as rights or licensing agreements. For more information or to have Amin speak at your event contact him at authoraminsalahuddin@gmail.com

Editor: Safiya Maryam Bint Arif, Mel Cohen
Cover and Interior Design: Megan Leid
Proof Reader: Tracy Johnson
Publishing Advisor: Mel Cohen Inspired Authors Press
       https://inspiredauthorspress.com
Publisher: Leaders 2 Leadership, LLC https://12lgroup.com

Website: https://www.aminsalahuddin.com
Facebook: https://www.facebook.com/AuthorAminSalahuddin
Twitter: @AuthorAminSalah
LinkedIn: https://www.linkedin.com/company/AuthorAminSalahuddin
Instagram: @AuthorAminSalahuddin

Printed in the United States of America

# CONTENTS

# DEDICATION

This book is dedicated to my daughters, Muntaha, Yusra, and Sara. You have been a true blessing and inspiration for me to continue to find the purpose of my life. You are my beautiful, loving, caring, supportive, intelligent, patient, humble, obedient, respectful, and everything positive children.

My hope is that you will view this book as an opportunity to learn from my experiences and build on them. As you grow older and encounter new obstacles, remember that such hurdles can be overcome with patience, perseverance, and determination. My advice for you is to keep your faith in Allah and always remember that He knows best. My love for you is unconditional, and I wish all the success for you in this world and hereafter.

# ACKNOWLEDGMENTS

A special thanks to my wife, Safiya, and daughters, Muntaha, Yusra, and Sara, who adapted to my entrepreneurial journeys and the struggles that accompanied them. I am so grateful for my wife's support and all the sacrifices she made throughout our struggles while raising our children.

I am very grateful for having Dr. Khawar Sheikh as my friend. I have known Khawar since his student life. He is a visionary, a great friend, and a savior of my vision of launching a nonprofit healthcare system. He didn't hesitate to offer his support when I told him about my dream of opening a nonprofit community health center.

Many thanks to Nameir Majette. He is a dear friend and a subject matter expert in healthcare administration who has dedicated his career to helping healthcare organizations improve their operations. When I asked Nameir for financial support and hours upon hours of donated time, without hesitation, he committed to both.

I am truly grateful to Nirav Gohel, the brains behind the technology. Nirav has become one of the leading experts in the field of technology implementation. I appreciate his support, commitment, and positive can-do attitude.

Thanks to Scott Buchannan. Scott is a leader by birth! He is the strategist and the visionary. When Texas opted out of Medicaid expansion, Scott supported my idea of a private-sector solution to solve the problem. I am grateful for his friendship and leadership.

A very special thanks to Islam Mossaad, Sunita Murti, Cristal Finke, Dr. Faris Hashim, Dr. Sadia Rashid, Dr. Tariq Malik, Dr. Durreshahwar Khan, Dr. Emran Rouf, Dr. Imtiyaz Hakeem and Manal Abdulkareem for volunteering their time at Eixsys Healthcare System.

I owe a huge thank you to Laura McManus, Zahir Walji, and all my friends who have supported me in my business development efforts. I appreciate all the time and energy they put in and am eternally grateful for their help.

# ABOUT THE AUTHOR

Amin is one of nine children born to Indian immigrants who migrated to the United States from Pakistan, ultimately residing in Round Rock, Texas.

In 1978 Amin's father was offered a job at Heathrow Airport. As a result, he and his family relocated to London, England, where Amin started kindergarten at age four.

From London, the family moved to Karachi, Pakistan. Then in the mid-1980s, they slowly migrated to New York, where Amin finished his high school education. In 1994 Amin moved to Toronto, Canada, and completed his undergraduate degree in Computer Information Systems.

Amin married in 2003 and is the father of three beautiful daughters. He is an entrepreneur, a nonprofit healthcare founder, and a servant leader. Listening to community needs and finding innovative ways to serve has always been part of Amin's passion, vision, and mission.

By education and profession, Amin is a software engineer. As a small business owner, he has built up a vast network of customers and associates who are loyal to him because of his professionalism and commitment to excellence.

He is also a firm believer in giving back to those around him, especially when it comes to helping others less fortunate than himself. As a result, he founded Eixsys Healthcare System in 2014 and devoted his time to volunteering and establishing this nonprofit healthcare organization.

Amin is passionate about helping others succeed by providing guidance and advice when needed. His goal is to assist others in achieving their dreams and aspirations by providing them with tools to reach their goals and objectives.

Amin was named the Investor of the Year by the Round Rock Chamber of Commerce in 2016. In addition, he served on several boards, including the Round Rock Chamber of Commerce (2016–2021) and the Round Rock Police Foundation (2018–2021). He is an alumnus of the Leadership Round

Rock Class of 2016, where he learned the importance of civic engagement and local leadership.

Once he earned his Master's degree, Amin still searched for more knowledge in his field. While writing his dissertation to earn a Doctorate in Business Administration, he shifted from academics to finding a technology solution to Healthcare Interoperability. From that moment on, his focus turned to the fast-moving field of computer technology related to healthcare.

# FOREWORD

I first met Amin when I spoke at a Leadership Round Rock class graduation while I was serving as the Commanding General of the 36th Infantry Division prior to my retirement from the Army.

I was impressed by the passion and leadership style he has shown with his tech company, and by the innovation he demonstrated when he launched a nonprofit private sector healthcare solution for the uninsured.

As I've gotten to know Amin, I'm further impressed by his driving desire to serve his community as a leader. His continued service on the Round Rock Chamber of Commerce board and Police Foundation as well as always seeking other opportunities to serve his community demonstrate that he is truly a servant leader.

**Major General (Ret.)**
**Patrick Hamilton**

I have known Amin since tenth grade in our John Bowne High School, Queens, New York. Amin was polite and always willing to help everyone. I recall when he laid down his life for a friend and ended up in the hospital. He was always a cheerful and dependable friend. Amin put into jeopardy all the hard work and achievements that took him years to obtain. I hope that his wonderful and simple book is a success.

We have options about the work we do and the role it plays in our lives. But it's precisely here that so many of us get fixed. With so many options, we battle to figure out what we really want or where to start. A Path to Learning, Perseverance, Building Resilience, and Impacting Your Community by Amin Salahuddin provides a small structure for discerning our calling and maximizing our impact.

An amazing read. I think we can all relate to this story on one level or another. I recommend this true and honest book to anyone. Thank you so much for writing this book. You are an incredible friend and inspiration.

**Dean, Rutgers University**
**Shaheen Fatima**

# INTRODUCTION

I will share my stories of perseverance toward achieving my goals and how my view of life transformed after going through three life-and-death experiences, a brutal jury trial, and surviving three business disasters.

Through my personal stories, I hope to inspire you to face your challenges head-on, persevere to overcome them, and become resilient. In this book I will share with you how I handled the challenges I encountered through the "Give First, Take Last," and "Forgive First" approach.

I will never forget the day, as it is forever embedded in my memory: a misty London morning in January of 1981, playing hide and seek with my siblings and beloved Uncle Naeem. Yet, little did I know that this joyous moment would soon give way to a life-threatening tragedy when an oncoming vehicle suddenly struck me down. Even at seven years old, nothing could erase that unforgettable experience of pain and suffering caused by one careless act.

It was Uncle Naeem's turn to count. I went out into the street to hide behind the car. Uncle Naeem spotted me and saw a high-speed car that lost control coming toward me. He screamed, "Amin, move!" but it was too late. The impact caused the worst pain I had ever felt in my short life—until I passed out.

**God has a purpose for you in life.**

At the hospital, my parents were told that I would not live another day once life support was removed. Thus, funeral plans were made. The grave was ordered to be dug and awaited the body of a young boy who had not yet experienced life. But by a God-given miracle, I was given a second chance to live, and my breath returned to me when the many life support measures were removed. As I was being released from the hospital, in my heart and my head, I vividly remember the words of the nurse who said, "God has a purpose for you in life." Those words were etched in my mind forever.

Later, as a teenager, I started to reflect and speculate on my life's purpose. From my faith in God's perspective, the purpose of life is nothing but to worship God. Worshiping God can also be achieved through performing good deeds in this world. Therefore, everything we do in our lives should be to please God and gain His love, mercy, and forgiveness. I knew this and believed it wholeheartedly.

I was overcome with the realization that life is precious, and we are given one opportunity to make the best of it. It's like being handed one last chance, and it's my responsibility to ensure that every moment counts! Although still unsure about which path to take, I was filled with determination and joy, knowing there were infinite possibilities ahead of me, all just waiting for me to find them.

As a youth growing up, I always wondered what I could give or what I could help with when I had nothing to offer. Initially, I related "giving" to only money but soon understood that time is by far

xxiv     GIVE FIRST, TAKE LAST

the most precious commodity. By engaging in service through volunteerism, I realized that even when I didn't feel like I had many material possessions to offer, simply dedicating a few hours each week made a huge difference. No matter how small the act may seem, every little effort counts and can have a positive ripple effect within our communities.

> No matter how small the act may seem, every little effort counts and can have a positive ripple effect within our communities.

As I matured, the complexities of life became more apparent. Everyone has a different mindset and method for achieving their goals. While an employee's paycheck reflects consistent effort, a nimble investor will leverage market movements to secure profits. Even grifters and robbers have strategies in which they gamble with risk to steal money. Yet, each person is unique, much the same as no two fingerprints are alike!

Since childhood I wanted to become an entrepreneur so I could do more to give back and do good in this world. I would play games with my siblings related to the supply chain, trades, and tolls that involved profit and loss. Early on, they began calling me "the businessman." It felt good!

My life journey has faced many challenges including two more near-death experiences and a brutal jury trial. I lost my savings three times on three different business startups before I became a successful entrepreneur.

I learned early on that facing a challenge and overcoming it made me stronger and better able to handle future bumps in the road. It begins by knowing who my sources of support are when my ideas and implementation are not going as planned.

One big lesson I have learned is that life can be unpredictable, but it is possible to break through the most demanding challenges with resilience and optimism. I started to embrace positivity, despite the unexpected hardships I faced. These experiences taught me that my spirit would never give way to defeat!

I found support from my wife, my family, friends, professionals, and my connection to God. I embraced the support from others. Having someone to talk to made a big difference in how well I coped with the challenges.

Some people cope by talking to friends or family, while others cope by journaling, meditating, or praying. I chose to face few challenges head-on *(and there were plenty!).*

I have persistently worked on my childhood business startup ideas since I was a teenager. My resilience kept me going after my first two businesses failed. Once I became a husband and father, I continued my journey toward establishing my business ideas. Thanks to my wife, I was fortunate that I was able to keep 99 percent of my attention on my work and consistently move forward.

Building resilience is an important skill, as it allows you to endure life's challenges and triumph over them. One way to build resilience is to understand that difficulties can lead to growth. The key is to maintain a positive outlook, because at a time of needed resilience, what matters most is how we react and adapt.

Time is fleeting, so why not make the most of your wealth while you can? Life's too short to squander away opportunities and resources—put them to good use now rather than letting them slip through your

**Building resilience is an important skill, as it allows you to endure life's challenges and triumph over them.**

fingers. Giving back is one of the key ingredients to a prosperous society. When we give, we help make the world a better place for everyone. Sometimes we overlook the importance of having an attitude of *Giving First* and *Taking Last*.

*Giving First:* **Give all you can and take nothing or expect nothing in return**. This is the secret to a prosperous society.

*Taking Last:* **Do not expect anything in return when you give or provide for others. You will be blessed for** *Giving First*.

> **Remember, every life has its challenges, purposes, beginning, and end. How you live yours and what you leave behind is in your hands.**

When we give intending to help others, we open ourselves up to limitless possibilities. We become more compassionate, loving, and connected to those around us. As a result, we create a community full of abundance and prosperity. The good just follows without us asking or taking anything.

Through practicing my belief of *Give First, Take Last*, and *Forgive First*, I became resilient in facing life's challenges.

Everyone who has lived an adult life has faced challenges, whether it was something that threatened their physical well-being or challenged their beliefs. I argue that we build resilience through these challenges, but only if we learn from these setbacks instead of allowing them to bring us down.

After the success of my third business venture, I continued giving back, but this time through a mission-driven nonprofit healthcare organization named Eixsys Healthcare System https://www.ehsclinic.org/ (EHS). EHS builds bridges between faith-based community centers and underserved communities through access to primary medical care.

Remember, every life has its challenges, purposes, beginning, and end. How you live yours and what you leave behind is in your hands.

Follow along with me as I search the depths of my soul to uncover the meaning behind life. Along this journey, you'll discover challenges, setbacks, and victories alike, all courageously conquered by yours truly! So, let's embark on an exciting exploration together, and you will see how powerful a purposeful path can be.

# CHAPTER 1

# DEVELOPING POSITIVE THINKING

Perhaps the biggest obstacle to building resilience is having a negative mindset. A positive outlook on life is essential for achieving success and building resilience. Just as a lack of light will prevent plants from growing, negative thoughts will prevent you from reaching your full potential. When you allow negative thoughts to take root, they will quickly multiply and spread, causing you to feel overwhelmed and hopeless. However, just as a room can be filled with light by opening the curtains, your mind can be filled with positive thoughts by making a conscious effort to do so, which will involve surrounding yourself with positive people, attending self-development lectures, reading inspiring stories, or all of the above. By taking steps to fill your mind with positive thoughts, you can create a bright future for yourself.

Unfortunately, negativity seeps through as we experience life. We can counter that negativity by developing a positive outlook which allows us to see the best in people and situations. For some, this comes by experiencing the love of our families, parents, guardians, grandparents, extended family members, and friends. For many, faith strengthens the sense of hope and possibility. They come to see God as a loving force that is always with them, no matter what challenges they face. For others, removing negativity may come from different sources: perhaps nature or art or simply being kind to others. Removing negativity is essential for leading a happy and fulfilling life.

## REMOVING NEGATIVITY

If you are serious about removing negativity from your life, you must ask yourself, "How can I view negative life experiences from a positive perspective?"

One way to do this is to focus on the lessons learned from these experiences. Another way is to appreciate that you took a chance at something. Don't let your failures define you; take time to strategize and try again. Understanding and processing the experience will make you stronger and more resilient. Most people don't make the same mistake twice. It is possible to find light even in the darkest of times. In fact, the light becomes stronger with each positive action you take. Know that!

> **How can I view negative life experiences from a positive perspective?**

If you're going to overcome adversity, misfortune, and distress; if you want to improve your life and relationships with others, then don't point your finger at one person, incident, or setback—it's usually the combination of circumstances, available resources, attitudes, and actions that will make the difference.

In times of my difficulties, I gave first—*Give without expecting anything in return.* When we give our time, money, or both, we receive an uplift in our spirit. It is human nature to help others, but sometimes we are caught in our predicament and don't think of doing this. I find that ironic because it has been scientifically proven that the more we give, the better we feel. The feeling builds and builds and provides a peaceful contentment in our lives.

We can all see negative experiences from a positive perspective when we choose to do so.

## THINKING POSITIVE

The famous Urdu language poet, Dr. Allama Iqbal, wrote in his book,

**"tundī-e-bād-e-mukẖālif se na ghabrā ai uqaab,**
**ye to chaltī hai tujhe ūñchā uḌāne ke liye"**

*This roughly translates as, "Don't Fear the Intensity of the Headwind, O' Falcon, It Only Blows to Help you Fly Even Higher."*

No matter who we are or where we come from, life is full of challenges. Whether dealing with a difficult work situation, navigating a tricky relationship, or getting through a rough patch, we all have our fair share of challenges. And while some challenges may seem insurmountable at first, remember they are often tests designed to make us stronger and more resilient. So instead of running away from challenges, why not embrace them and see what you can become? After all, the only way to overcome life's challenges is to face them head-on. Then who knows—you might surprise yourself with what you can achieve.

When you let go of all expectations of what you need and focus on what you can give first, you attain the ultimate victory over personal desires. I know this is challenging behavior, but it is not impossible.

## FEELING CONTENT

When you let go of your desires for things like money or success or whatever else you think will make you happy and instead focus on giving to others, there's no doubt in my mind that you will be more content than ever! In my life, the more I give, the more I feel blessed, and with that comes contentment, a feeling of peace from God beyond all understanding.

Author Frank Annenberg says this, "When you give something with strings attached, your focus is on how you'll benefit personally. On the other hand, when you give of yourself without expecting something in return, your entire focus is on pleasing the recipient. You're not really giving if you expect something in return."

Getting caught up in your life and what you want to achieve is easy. You can focus so much on your personal goals and expectations that you forget about the people around you. However, if you take the time to think about others and what you can do for them, you may find that you can reach your own goals faster. When you focus on giving back, you create a positive feedback loop that benefits everyone involved. You not only make progress toward your own goals, but you also help others to achieve theirs.

So next time you feel stressed or overwhelmed by your expectations, take a step back and consider what you can do for someone else. It will make all the difference in the world. For example, if you are searching for a job, you can do it alone, or create a group of people that fall in the same category to teach and learn new approaches.

## BOTTLENECK TRAITS

You might not realize it, but the traits that hold you back are in your head.

Here are a few examples of what I am talking about:

1. Negative self-talk: "I'm not smart enough; I'm not pretty enough; I'm too fat; I'm too thin; I'm not tall enough; I'm too tall."

2. Procrastination: "I'll work on it later" and never get to it. Starting something and not finishing it. "I'm too busy right now," and it never gets done.

3. Perfectionism: Setting standards too high.

Perfectionism is having everything perfect before moving to the next step. In business, this can lead to bankruptcy. Let's learn from one of the world's largest companies, Microsoft. They often release a new product or service and have several updates or fixes within months. They do not wait around for their competition to release something before them.

If you are someone who wants to learn how to get rid of negativity, face the fear that comes with change, and be courageous in taking responsibility to become everything you want to be, then keep reading.

## GIVING

Anything you give falls under two categories: replaceable assets and irreplaceable assets. Replaceable assets are mainly tangible assets such as money, material, real estate, or objects you can quickly associate with a price tag. Irreplaceable assets—such as volunteering time, sharing intellectual property, having knowledge, practicing goodwill, and seeing how you can be an asset to others are intangible.

Giving contributes toward building an economic ecosystem and *Giving First* is fundamental to thriving societies. Communities that understand the fundamentals behind "Give First" develop and flourish better socio-economically, versus communities that complain, constantly criticize, and look to receive only opportunities.

When it comes to money, there are many misconceptions: It's not about how much you make; it is about what percent you give back and how much you save. But there is also something else: money isn't just something that happens in your bank account or wallet. Instead, you create something by doing what makes sense for your life—you decide what works for you. Money is the byproduct of your education, hard work, perseverance, and success.

To give without expecting a return is a positive maxim. Don't expect any return, benefits, or favors when you give. That is what sincere giving is all about.

In Islam, there is a concept called "Infaq", which is giving for charity, not expecting a return, and giving all one can after meeting one's basic needs. I have always tried to live up to that standard.

In Christianity, "...*let each one give as he pur-poses in his heart, not grudgingly or of necessity; for God loves a cheerful giver*" *(2 Corinthians 9:7).*

Hinduism also preaches giving. "*In vain does the mean man acquire food; it is – I speak the truth – verily his death; he who does not cherish a comrade or a friend, who eats all alone, is all sin*" *(Rig Veda 10.117.1-2,6).*

When you give first in a society where the majority expects to get first, your "give first" will be like striking a hammer on a huge rock. Yes, you will not see the impact on the first strike, but with con-tinuous effort, others will join. Eventually, the ham-mer will crack the rock. Therefore, you need moti-vation or a motive to continue the momentum of giving first.

Giving is the spark that ignites a beneficial chain reaction. Even simple acts of kindness can have far-reaching, positive effects on both giver and receiver alike!

# CHAPTER 2

# REMOVING FEAR AND LIVING A LIFE OF PURPOSE

Living in New York City was another life experience. When I was fourteen years old, my parents left my older brother and me under the care of my father's close friend. Although the rampant crime in the city was not the best environment for a young teenager, I made some good friends at school and at the Masjid (the place of worship for Muslims) and wholeheartedly enjoyed their company.

New York was one of the worst cities in the late 80s and early 90s. People were frequently mugged, and it was a general understanding to keep a few dollars in your pocket to give to the muggers when attacked.

> **But, of course, there is a better way: a life of giving, not taking from others.**

At age sixteen, I was five feet seven inches and weighed around ninety-five pounds. I also wore glasses from the '70s. One evening in October of 1990, returning from work in the Bronx, New York, I had five dollars in my pocket when two muggers approached me. I gave the five dollars to one of them, but the other punched my eyes, crushing my eyeglasses on my face. I was rushed to the hospital and had eleven stitches surrounding my left eye.

I came to understand that many of these criminals felt that they had been deprived by what they viewed as institutional discrimination and didn't see the opportunity to get out of their vicious cycle of earning their livelihood through criminal activities.

But, of course, there is a better way: a life of giving, not taking from others.

## USING FEAR FOR SELF-DEVELOPMENT

My life mission and goal have remained very strong. I believe God gifted me with a second chance at life, a miracle. The fear of death doesn't reside in my heart and mind. Instead, I believe that death only comes to people when it is their time.

Fear is a deeply ingrained emotion within our human nature. It is what keeps us safe from harm, and it is what drives us to act in the face of danger. However, fear can also be a powerful force for evil.

**Fear is what politicians use to divide and conquer their citizens**

Fear keeps people apart and prevents them from getting to know one another's similarities and appreciating their differences.

Fear makes people violent and forces them to disregard the suffering of those who seem different.

Fear is what politicians use to divide and conquer their citizens. Fear can lead people to make bad decisions that are not in their best interests, such as living in a state of constant insecurity rather than facing the unknown somewhere else with a positive outlook.

Many of us go through life without really living. We exist in a state of constant fear, afraid to take risks or step out of our comfort zones. We tell ourselves that it's better to play it safe, to stay within the confines of what we know. But what if we could choose to live differently, more freely?

**Instead of allowing fear to paralyze you, use it as motivation to move closer to the life you want to live.**

What if we could remove our fear and live a purposeful life, not allowing it to control us and becoming free to pursue our dreams and goals? We can follow our passion and live with purpose. Life is too short to waste living in fear. Live boldly, without regret or hesitation!

Fear of change, fear of rejection, fear of failure, fear of getting injured, losing valuables, or being attacked can be as paralyzing as the fear of the unknown and very often prevents us from taking risks. So instead of seeing fear as a negative emotion that should be avoided, learn to use fear as a guide. Instead of allowing fear to paralyze you, use it as motivation to move closer to the life you want to live.

Fear is usually an excellent indicator that there's something about the situation that makes us uncomfortable. Embrace that feeling. After all, it's only when we step outside of our comfort zone that we can grow and change.

**Embrace your fear and see where it takes you.**

So next time you feel fear, use it as a sign that you're on the right path instead of letting it hold you back. Embrace your fear and see where it takes you. You might be surprised by what you find. You are braver than you think you are!

## BUILDING CONFIDENCE

Here are seven steps to help you build your confidence as you face challenges or setbacks.

1. Stop comparing yourself to others.

2. Celebrate and reflect on your wins.

3. Embrace your failures and view them as learning opportunities.

4. Practice gratitude.

5. Surround yourself with positive thinkers.

6. Continue to step out of your comfort zone

7. Be who you are.

It took me years to overcome my fear of losing my dream of becoming an entrepreneur and refocus my life after my first business venture right out of high school fell through.

It wasn't easy to overcome the negativity I felt. Finally, I began to take action and listen to lectures on positive thinking and leadership development. I focused on what had gone well rather than what did not go well and comparing myself with others. I reflected on how I reached the point where I was able to launch my first business. I picked up lessons from this failed business venture. I felt grateful for the faith that kept me going during this difficult time. I surrounded myself with an encouraging community of people at a local Masjid before continuing with my college studies. It took me some time and more rigorous planning, but eventually I took another chance at fulfilling my dreams.

From the age of eight, I always wanted to be an entrepreneur, so even my childhood games with siblings were related to making a profit. As I got older, I knew I wanted to work and save up seed money for my first real business. While in high school, I worked several jobs seven days a week. I worked at a grocery store and a dry cleaner after school and delivered the *New York Times* and *Pennysaver* coupon booklets door to door at 3 AM in the mornings.

While it was challenging, especially when I was tired after a long day of school, I felt the struggle was worth it because I looked forward to my dream turning into a reality.

One afternoon about a week after my bandages

were removed from above my eyes, where I had stitches from being punched and having my eyeglasses crushed in my face, I called my dear friend, Hamayoun Yusufi, to go with me to purchase new glasses. As we entered the optometry store, a robber came in right behind us, put his gun on Hamayoun's head, and demanded everyone empty their pockets and the optometrist empty his cash register.

I didn't empty my pocket, as I needed the money for my glasses! I faced death but was not about to give in to the robber, until he pointed the gun at me. He shouted for me to give him my wallet. I feared losing the money, so I was holding out, but when the gun was point blank in my face, I took out my wallet and threw it at him. The mugger instantly pulled the trigger in response to my frustration and anger. As I watched the cylinder of the gun slowly turn, I felt my life was about to come to an end.

Thank God the bullet was not in the chamber, and as the robber loaded his gun, I quickly apologized, picked up the wallet, and handed it to him. Pulling the trigger panicked everyone. The robber then pointed the gun at the cashier and cleaned out the cash register; my second brush with death.

After the robbery at the optometry store, I was shaken up. In my mind, over and over, I could see the gun's cylinder turn slowly as the trigger was pulled, believing that in a few seconds I would be killed. I never considered that something like this could happen in broad daylight. I was so grateful that Hamayoun was there with me. He was calm and helped me stay calm.

After the robber left, the New York Police arrived, viewed the video recording, took our statements, and promised they would do everything to find the robber and bring him to justice. But, of course, they never caught him, a norm in New York City. Back then every day countless criminal cases like these were reported and never solved.

This entire experience of repeatedly being mugged was disheartening. Still, I immediately returned to work—not just to keep my dream alive, but also because I needed to work to have the finances to support my expenses. Due to my circumstances, I learned the valuable lesson of being resilient and staying persistent.

> **The past is the past, and you can't change it. The only thing you can do is pick up some lessons from your experiences and move on.**

Being one of the few minorities in school can be tough, but I found strength and comfort within a small circle of close friends. We talked to each other about our struggles. The situations we endured had us drawing closer together and creating a bond unlike any other. Because I used to walk home from school every day, it took a few more beatings, muggings, and dangerous situations before my friends suggested I learn Taekwondo to empower myself and defend against any adversaries lurking around the corner. I took their advice and worked hard to receive my brown belt. I used fear as my motivation to create a successful outcome. Earning a brown belt in Taekwondo was a huge boost in my confidence.

# CHAPTER 3

# MOVE ON— STOP LIVING IN THE PAST

The past is the past, and you can't change it. The only thing you can do is pick up some lessons from your experiences and move on. It is okay to be upset about what happened in the past,

**The past is the past, and you can't change it. The only thing you can do is pick up some lessons from your experiences and move on.**

but not okay to dwell on it. Instead, move on and start fresh with new experiences that will make you happy again!

## SETTING GOALS, BEING PERSISTENT, AND LEARNING LESSONS

Life can be a struggle. It brings many physical, emotional, and mental challenges, but the key is never giving in. Challenges, if we allow them, make us stronger and help us reach higher life goals.

I grew up watching my parents pray five times daily, which made me a frequent visitor at the Masjid. Living next to the Flushing Muslim Center in New York helped move me forward and get me through some tough times. I frequently attended for prayers and listened to sermons and lectures on forgiveness in Islam by Dr. Israr Ahmed and Yusuf Islahi, great scholars and educators. The messages were very often about forgiveness, as only forgiveness helps you forget and cleanses your heart of bitterness. When you forgive, you move on, leaving that bitterness and resentment, pain, and anger behind.

Sincerely forgiving someone allows you to find closure, which frees your mind and soul and ultimately enables you to move on in life in a better direction.

I was told to give "Sadaqa" (charity) and thank God for saving my life and keeping me in His protection. From a strictly religious perspective, giving charity is not just a way to help the needy and earn God's pleasure, but it is also a way of showing gratitude to God.

Practicing gratitude by reflecting upon the blessings and favors that God bestowed upon me is how I found my ultimate peace and the courage and confidence to move on.

Whenever you have doubts about your mission, revisit why you are on the path you are on and rededicate yourself to fulfilling your undertaking.

We've all been there: we come home from work exhausted from a long day of dealing with difficult people and situations, even sulking because it's too much for our minds and bodies to handle. We are just looking for some time to unwind after a stressful day. In those moments, how do you view your experiences that day? Allow yourself to see each of those negative, stressful moments as an opportunity for growth. It won't be easy at first, but persistence in thinking this way will readjust your former pattern of feeling too overwhelmed to do anything about it.

When faced with your next challenge, ask, *"What lessons will be learned from this situation? How will this challenge help me better prepare for future challenges like this one? Will this experience help me grow into someone more resilient?"* These questions are critical. They will help guide your decisions as you move forward.

My experiences in life started shaping my mind at a very early age. I wanted to live a life of value, helping and serving the community and especially the underserved. At that point in my life, I didn't know how to give when I didn't have much myself. I was working on overcoming my PTSD due to a handful of traumatizing experiences, and forgiving those who created the trauma was paramount to my healing. If I wanted to serve others and have a pur-poseful life, I had to go forward with love in my heart—for everyone.

As a high school student, I didn't have much to give, so I found ways to volunteer my time by either distributing clothes and food to the needy or helping in the construction project at the Flushing Muslim Center. Giving a few hours each week made a huge difference in my life.

Attending high school, hanging out with friends, working full time, and then finding time to volunteer was very difficult to manage, but I learned early on that I must make sacrifices for my life's dreams

**You can't always have what you want, but you can always do whatever it takes to get it!**

to come true. Think of it this way: You can't always have what you want, but you can always do whatever it takes to get it! One of the many life lessons that would guide me in future years.

As a successful business owner, I appear to have it all together. Fear of the unknown and fear of failure held me back after my second business failed. It wasn't easy to take a risk and quit my job to start a business.

I was married by this time, and we had two young children, ages five and three. I also feared public speaking, but I have learned to overcome that fear. I've learned that fear can be paralyzing, but it can also be an excellent motivator. I couldn't fail this time. I had a family to raise. I discovered we, indeed, are more potent than our fear.

> **I've learned that fear can be paralyzing, but it can also be an excellent motivator.**

The Roman writer, Virgil, wrote, *"Fortune favors the bold."* That is another lesson I have learned over the years. If we do not take chances and act boldly, fewer opportunities will present themselves, and the possibilities for success will not be as great. But as you will see, I often took chances and learned important lessons from them.

# CHAPTER 4

# CONSEQUENCES OF DECISIONS MADE BASED ON EMOTIONS

We all know that feeling of being caught up in the moment when our emotions take over, and we make a decision that we later regret. In the heat of the moment, it can be difficult to think clearly and make rational choices, as we are often confused. When in an emotional frame of mind, not only do the chances of making wrong decisions increase, but we often leave ourselves vulnerable and allow someone else to take advantage of us.

How often has someone else convinced you to buy something you didn't need? I distinctly remember when my friend went to a dealership and ended up leasing a Toyota Sienna, a large SUV that seats up to eight. The van was just for him and his wife. He, of course, ended up breaking the lease that week and lost approximately $5K in the process.

## CONTROLLING EMOTIONS

When you are caught up in your emotions, take a step back and think about what you're doing and revisit the topic and decision-making later. Whether this is a situation where you must respond in person or to a phone call or email request, react slowly in making a decision. Don't allow anyone to exploit your emotions or take advantage of your vulnerability. Instead, ask yourself, "*Is this a decision I'll be happy with later, or am I just being impulsive?*" If you can learn to control your emotions and make better decisions, others will be less likely to take advantage of you.

It is natural to feel emotional sometimes, but many of us regularly allow our emotions to override our rational thoughts. It becomes challenging to think clearly when emotions far exceed reason. Decisions made at the height of emotion are more commonly harmful to you and others. We may lash out in anger or make impulsive decisions that we later

**If you can learn to control your emotions and make better decisions, others will be less likely to take advantage of you.**

regret. Emotions and reasons must be a healthy balance in order to make good decisions.

It is essential to keep our emotions in check because some people and most media can manipulate a person's emotions; you can believe something completely false. Researching and thinking through all the facts before making decisions is paramount to your success.

I attended a lecture by Dr. Qazi Javed, a psychiatrist. In one word, he explained the difference between action and reaction, and that word is pause. Quick, impulsive decisions can create negative consequences. Reacting without thinking through all the possibilities may lead to disappointment. I speak from experience. My venture into the business of supermarkets did not have the outcome I expected. In hindsight, upon examining my decisions and actions, I realized there were many gaps in my understanding of the process.

I learned that emotions are an important part of decision-making but should be used only as guideposts—not as final determinants.

When I reflect on my emotional attachment to the $250 for the pair of eyeglasses I was about to purchase, I realize my instant reaction toward the robber could have caused my death. Instead, all I was thinking about was that I really needed the glasses to see the board in the classroom. Even by sitting in the front row, things were blurry. Not having the glasses was giving me a headache, and I was not able to focus in class; I was falling behind. Even so, I forgot in that moment what was important—not the glasses at all—it was my safety and the safety of those around me who were also experiencing the same trauma.

By the age of seventeen, I had already survived three life-and-death experiences. What I gave up on was not my mission but the idea that instead of starting my business in New York, I would move to Toronto, Canada, and launch my first business venture there. It took one more brush with death before I finally moved to Toronto.

The final situation that scarred me and ultimately convinced me to leave New York for Toronto was when I saw a girl being harassed by two bullies. I reacted as a first responder and jumped in to help her. One guy took out his Rambo-style knife and shouted, "Back-off!" After a short pause, I responded, "No! Leave her alone!"

The guy chased after me, poised with his knife to hurt or kill me. I used the self-defense skills I learned in Taekwondo to bring him down. The onlookers who didn't do anything to help me now came and surrounded me, cheering wildly. When I thought everything was over and the girl had gotten away, I made the classic mistake that any self-defense expert will tell you not to make. I gave the knife back to the bully. I didn't want any long-time trouble with this guy and thought that was the right thing to do.

After that, I crossed the road and started walking home. I should have watched my back. The defeated bully came from behind and stabbed me in the left side of my jaw. Doctors said if the knife had hit one centimeter lower, it would have skipped the bone, cut my throat, and I would have died instantly.

First responders, such as police, paramedics, and firefighters, put their lives on the line daily to protect and save those in need. They must possess courage, leadership skills, a sense of responsibility for their actions, and the ability to face all consequences that may come from their actions. Unfortunately, even with all the preparation and dedication, there are still times when first responders can find themselves in dangerous situations.

There have been cases where paramedics and emergency physicians have been attacked by the very patients they were attempting to save or firefighters entering burning buildings to rescue those trapped inside. These brave individuals risk their lives every day to protect and serve others, and they deserve all of our respect and admiration for doing so. The difference between a professional first responder and when I first responded to a call for help from the girl was my emotional reaction.

Living in New York City in the late 80s and early 90s, crime was an everyday reality. I finally decided to move on, as my mission was not to be a vigilante. My decision was final: to leave America on my own as soon as I turned eighteen, which was about a year away. My sister, who lived in Canada, sponsored me, and I was ready to leave the USA in less than a year. I made my decision to go, and I believe it saved my life.

## EMOTIONAL BUSINESS STARTUPS

When I was younger, I was one of many who chose emotions to push myself to work tirelessly to make money and start my own business. When I graduated from high school, I saved about $15,000. I worked three jobs, risked my life by coming back late at night, and risked my health by sleeping fewer hours than a teenager should sleep. I was so emotionally invested in my goal that I forgot about my surroundings and the people around me. Consequently, I developed a narrow focus. I hardly spent money on entertainment and improving my quality of life through having a good time. I created a fear of losing money and it started to damage my socioeconomic circle.

According to Zapier.com, roughly three in five Americans (61 percent) have had an idea for starting a business, and around a third (34 percent) have had more than one. But an overwhelming majority of those people—92 percent—didn't follow through with turning their business idea into a reality.

When people launch or first consider starting a business, they have different emotions and planned out goals. They know what they want to do but do not always know how. Nevertheless, their thoughts are optimistic, not considering everything that can go wrong in the beginning stages of starting a business.

However, these emotions of definite easy success eventually fade away, and the person moves on to the second stage in the progression of the business. In this stage, they are no longer thinking about what they want to do but how to achieve it. They also become more realistic about potential obstacles and how long it will take to overcome them.

The first business I launched was the import and export of garments. I contacted garment manufacturers in Pakistan and asked for samples of quality knitted golf shirts, sweatshirts, and pants. I took the pieces to stores and, in a few weeks, secured an order for 5,000 knitted golf shirts.

I was attempting my first experience in business by launching without a partner or a mentor. I learned many lessons related to the shipment: freight, customs, bill of lading, the release of the order, and much more. Finally, after three months, the merchandise arrived. The first opportunity to multiply my investment had begun, and the chance to launch a nonprofit organization was about to begin.

When I opened the first box, I was shocked. All of the clothing was subpar—the kind that most stores would have rejected.

I quickly opened the second box and then a third. My heart sank. All the clothing was of poor quality, unlike the quality of the samples shown to potential clients. I quickly realized I had been conned. My decision was emotional; I fell for the rhetoric of my fellow countryman to support his manufacturing business in Pakistan. Since I had paid in advance and didn't execute a line of credit, which helps protect international trade, I lost my entire $15,000.

## EMOTIONAL BUSINESS EXIT

I now had 5,000 low-quality golf shirts in my possession. A big challenge was before me, as this was the second time I had lost my hard-earned money. I saw my lifelong dreams being crushed. That hard-earned $15,000 went to a dishonest person who didn't value or respect my dreams.

I had previously learned the importance of persistence, regardless of how difficult life's challenges become. I now had to deal with the next phase of my business: liquidating the defective shirts. I visited local flea markets and multiple vendors. Everyone wanted the golf shirts on consignment, which meant they would pay me after selling them.

I negotiated 50 percent of the inventory with Mr. Fausto, which is 2,500 golf shirts to be sold on consignment, with a $1,000 down payment. Mr. Fausto agreed to write a $450 check and requested that I return the next day for the other $550 to complete the down payment.

I selected Mr. Fausto from several vendors because he mentioned that he was a missionary in Nepal and talked about Prophet Isa (Jesus, son of Mary—peace be upon him). He sounded like the most trustworthy person, so the deal was made.

The next day, there was no sign of Mr. Fausto, and he was nowhere to be found for several weeks. Finally, after two weeks, his $450 check bounced.

It was like facing a financial calamity after a previous disaster. This betrayal left me in shock for several days. I was heartbroken. This brutal failure of my first business venture led me to focus more on my college education. I had just experienced first-hand the "dog-eat-dog world." I'd have to wait, plan, and save for another business launch.

Startups are not easy. Many times, people steal ideas and resources. However, without a business coach, mentor, or advisor, you may make quick decisions before fully thinking them through. That was the difficult lesson I learned from my first business experience. My initial desire to create a business was dreamed up through pure emotion and insufficient understanding of what it would take. Selling the defective inventory was also purely an emotional action. I reacted quickly to cut my losses without looking into other options. I learned a lot about myself and others through this ordeal.

## ACTION AND PLANNING

Anyone who has started a new business knows it is exciting and challenging. There is so much to do and learn, and it can be difficult to know where to begin. However, there are some basic steps that all new businesses should take. First, you need to define your business goals and objectives. What are you hoping to achieve with your new venture? Next, you need to create a business plan to help you to map out the steps you need to take to reach your goals. Finally, you must ensure you have the financial resources to get your business off the ground. These three steps will help

**A business plan is a document that outlines your company's overall vision, goals, and mission.**

you start on the right foot and set up your new business for success.

I want to emphasize the term "business plan." A business plan is a document that outlines your company's overall vision, goals, and mission. It will also include the steps you'll take to achieve those goals.

Writing a business plan can be daunting, especially if you've never completed one. Fortunately, there are many resources available to help you get started. One of the most important things you can do is to find someone who can provide guidance and support throughout the process; a friend or family member with business experience, a professional consultant, the Small Business Administration (SBA), or an online service such as Liveplan https://www.liveplan.com/

While hiring someone to help you with your business plan may add some cost, it is worth getting the expert advice and assistance you need. With the right help, you'll be well on your way to achieving your entrepreneurial dreams.

I would recommend consulting a business coach or mentor before starting any venture so that you will have a better chance of success. Search for a well-recommended business coach who has been through a few business cycles and has a history of success. The coach must possess legal and technical knowledge in setting up a business and guiding you toward resources for your specific needs. This would include setting up your business as a sole proprietor, LLC, corporation, etc., and advising you on how to operate it once it is up and running. This coach will also help you stay focused on your goals and ensure that everything runs smoothly throughout the process. You must be selective in your choice. This is something I practice in every new phase of business development, which helps me pivot during uncertain times.

Before starting a business, one must consider answering some basic questions. *Who do I want to be? What kind of person am I? What do I want to accomplish with my business? Will this business make money?* These are the questions you must answer because if you don't know where you're going, you will not know how and when to get there.

Once you know what kind of business you want to manage and run, it is time for research! First, find out what others have done in a similar business, which is called reverse engineering. For example, if someone has opened a restaurant before and has had great success, look at their website, visit their restaurant, taste the food, and observe the service staff. See what they do right and duplicate it.

Also, find someone unsuccessful at starting a restaurant and find out what they did wrong. It could be food quality, service, help, lack of capital, location, lack of vision, or many other facets of opening and operating a new restaurant. It will provide insight into mistakes you can avoid that often lead to failure, as about 60 percent of restaurants fail in their first year and up to 80 percent fail by year five.

It is also helpful to ask questions and listen carefully to what they say. Then, look at how they handle challenges in their business so you have answers to the many challenges of opening a restaurant.

When I was a teenager, I thought starting a business was the ultimate way to success; let me tell you, it is worth it! This is why: when you follow your passion and leave everything else behind, you learn that what matters most is making your dream happen, which makes all the difference in the world.

## ROOT OUT EMOTIONAL CONFLICTS

How often have you found yourself in a situation where someone says one thing, but their actions say something else? It happens more than you think. Don't be that person who talks a good talk, but doesn't back it up with action.

If you want people to take you seriously, let your actions speak louder than your words. It is easy to make empty promises, but much harder to follow through on them. So, the next time you decide to make a promise to

**If you want people to take you seriously, let your actions speak louder than your words.**

someone or an organization, or speak motivating statements over a microphone, ask yourself: *Am I willing and able to follow through?*

Being honest is important because it helps build trust. When you are honest with someone, they are more likely to trust and feel comfortable around you. Lying and breaking promises create mistrust and can damage relationships. Being honest helps prevent misunderstandings and miscommunication. If you're always truthful, then there's no need to worry about what you said or how it was interpreted. Honesty is simply the right thing to do. It is essential to be truthful, even when it is not easy.

Stop letting emotions cloud your judgment and start arming yourself with knowledge! Drawing from diverse sources of information will help you make smarter choices and build resilience to life's most significant challenges. Don't let opinions derail you—turn to facts and watch how much further they take you!

# CHAPTER 5

# THE IMPACT OF EMPOWERING YOUTH

Our children may be young, but they can participate in some important decision-making that can ultimately shape their future. For example, a child may decide to play a certain sport and end up being a high school soccer star, maybe even getting a scholarship to college. A young adult may research universities to attend and find herself receiving scholarship offers. Receiving and deciding on opportunities can have the best impact when it comes to empowering our youth. In like manner, when it comes to finding a suitable partner for marriage and companionship, they definitely need to be ready to make that right decision for themselves.

Certainly, the decision-making process should be undertaken with guidance from family members or experienced counselors; however, considering a young adult's unique perspective can often be invaluable in not only achieving better outcomes but also providing them with greater autonomy in life.

## YOUTH EMPOWERMENT BUILDS CONFIDENCE

Decisions are a part of everyday life. What to wear, what to eat, which task of the day is most important and should be tackled first. The list goes on and on. In successful families, including children in family matters is an integral part of the decision-making process. When children are given a say in what goes on in their lives, it builds a sense of trust and respect between them and their parents or guardians. It also allows them to develop a sense of ownership and responsibility for their actions.

Furthermore, it instills in them a belief that their opinions matter and that they are valuable family members. As a result, children who are included in decision-making are more likely to be well-adjusted and happy. They also tend to do better in school and their relationships with family and friends.

Many parents don't fully understand how much their children can contribute to decision-making. Children often have unique and purer perspectives than adults; they should be involved in decision-making as often as it seems appropriate.

You must consider your children's ages when speaking to them on a topic. Be mindful of the subject matter and understand they might not be as professional as those you work with, or your circle of friends. I often talk to my kids in the morning while driving them to school. I once asked my thirteen-year-old about key factors of

**Just like any skill, confidence is something that must be developed.**

economic development for our region. She thought-
fully responded that undeveloped land in a metropolitan area is one of the factors.

Unsurprisingly, families who practice this
approach develop confident children who will avail
more opportunities in the professional, business, or
political world as adults. They have more knowledge
of the business climate they are entering.

Just like any skill, confidence is something that
must be developed; and, just like any other skill, the
earlier you start working on it, the better. There are
a number of simple things you can do to help your
child develop this vital skill. Talking to your teenage
children and taking an interest in their thoughts and
ideas is a great place to start. Another good idea is to
encourage them to volunteer.

As their parent, remember to praise their efforts
without focusing too much on the end result, then
provide guidance for them to experience success.

When we empower children to make decisions
independently, they learn how to lead and practice
good judgment. Decision-making opportunities

teach children about their limitations and strengths. They also learn how to balance their own needs with the needs of others.

For example, we provided different school options for our daughters to pick from but left the final decision for them to select the one they felt would be best for their overall education and development. In the end, the children are the ones who attend so the final choice should be theirs. Giving your children a voice allows them to speak their mind constructively.

## INFLUENCE ON CHILDREN

The old saying is true; it takes a village to raise a child. It takes a community of people coming together and supporting a culture that ensures that every child has the opportunity to reach their

> Giving your children a voice allows them to speak their mind constructively.

full potential. By working together, we can create a brighter future for all our children. At the same time, parents and guardians cannot just blindly follow that saying. We don't live in a perfect imaginary world, but we can all join to improve it.

I remember my parents telling me that four groups of people would influence who I am as a person. These include relationships with family, friends, teachers, and strangers. Each of these groups would have a different level of influence on me and would help shape my character and personality.

Certainly, my family would have the most significant impact as they are the closest to me and have known me for the longest time. Friends would come next, as they are people that I choose to spend my time with and we share common interests. Teachers would be next, as they are experts in their field and can provide me with guidance and knowledge. Finally, strangers would be last, as they are people I do not know and who have no personal connection to me. However, even though we may not have a personal relationship, they can still influence me through their actions and words.

How intensely someone might affect us can also be categorized into four main sub-categories: permanent, long term, short term, and temporary.

Permanent influence is generally exerted by parents and guardians, while long-term influence is typically exerted by other family members and close friends. Short-term influence is generally exerted by teachers, classmates, and distant relatives. Finally, in very simplified and non-specific terms, temporary influence is generally exerted by strangers.

As a result of these conversations, I learned that it is critical to be aware of the different levels of influence I allow people to have on my life. This knowledge has helped me to build resilience toward maintaining the vision my parents had for me.

**I learned that it is critical to be aware of the different levels of influence I allow people to have on my life.**

# CHAPTER 6

# BALANCING COLLEGE AND AFTER COLLEGE LIFE

In 1993 when I turned nineteen, I moved from New York to Toronto, Canada. I became the head of the household and the primary breadwinner, not by choice but due to circumstances. Living with me were my four younger siblings and my mother. My father continued working in Pakistan because my older sister studied medicine at Dow Medical College in Karachi, Pakistan, and someone had to be with her. My father's earnings in Pakistani Rupees, which we would convert into Canadian dollars, would not suffice for two weeks of groceries.

At nineteen, this was a huge responsibility, not just because I was the primary financial source but also because I felt I had to be a mentor by example to my younger siblings on staying positive while facing life's challenges.

The beautiful memories of enjoying time in high school and being with friends started to be overshadowed by my new responsibilities. After my first business failure, I quickly began to focus more on my undergraduate studies to set a good example for my siblings about the importance of higher education. Higher education opens more doors of opportunity. I kept a night job throughout my college years as a security officer doing foot patrol in below-freezing temperatures on industrial sites. It was an easy job to get because hardly anyone wanted to work under those conditions.

My parents have always been a huge encouragement in my life and made me believe that if I put my mind to something and worked hard on it, it would surely come true. They are a blessing because they never gave up on me, even when I failed. My mom always encouraged me to work hard on my studies and told me there is no such thing as "impossible" when you want something bad enough. Her favorite saying was, "If you want something bad enough, then all things are possible." And she was right!

## SELF-MOTIVATED TO STRIVE

I worked at night in the freezing cold of Canada, attended college in the morning, slept in the afternoon, spent time with my siblings in the evening, and got ready for work at night for three consecutive years. My motivation and positive attitude were due to my parents keeping me involved in family discussions and their support in building resilience. I was encouraged by many to focus on myself and become self-centered. Because of my parent's strong teaching and values, I clearly understood how much influence I should allow these people to have on me.

I love feeling like I'm constantly pushing myself to improve. That's why I love a good challenge. It is important to always be moving forward, and challenges help me do that. They also force me to confront my fears and doubts. It can be scary to put yourself out there, but it's always worth it in the end. Every challenge is an opportunity to learn and grow; I am grateful for that.

I had always been drawn to DeVry University in Toronto, Canada, because it had a reputation for being a place where students can get ahead in their careers, and not just with a degree from DeVry, but with the experience and contacts they'll gain from their time there. DeVry used to advertise 100 percent guaranteed jobs in your field of study after getting a bachelor's degree. Most of the time, students had job offers before they graduated. The only condition was to maintain a minimum GPA of 3.5. I enrolled as a self-pay student, quickly became an over-performer student, and was hired by the University to tutor students between class breaks.

When I am facing tough times, I often think about how other people might be dealing with worse conditions than me. For example, you see people living with chronic pain or diseases and realize that you may not have it as bad as they do. Going through my grueling experiences, I may have been in a lot of pain, sometimes even physically, but I knew it was only temporary. Through this process of reflection, I gained some perspective on my situation. In addition, it helped me realize that, even though I was going through a tough time, there were people out there dealing with much worse.

The Prophet Muhammad (Peace be upon him) said, "If the Day of Resurrection were established upon one of you, while he has in his hand a sapling (small plant), then let him plant it." (Ahmad).

This positive perspective helped me overcome my difficulties and negativity and freed me to keep moving forward.

## LIVING A PURPOSEFUL LIFE

When you know exactly what your purpose is and how to get there, then you'll be able to overcome any obstacles that come your way. You can't let yourself get bogged down in the minutiae of small things when bigger issues are at stake. Don't let anything get in the way when you know something is important; working toward it will bring you closer to your purpose.

**This positive perspective helped me overcome my difficulties and negativity and freed me to keep moving forward.**

I was not the one to shy away from a challenge. So, whenever I'm given the opportunity to take on a new task, I don't hesitate. I don't doubt myself. If it's something I have zero knowledge about, no problem, I'll create my knowledge base. The only tools I need are determination and finding the right resources through individuals, the internet, or educational material.

Taking on a challenge can be terrifying, especially when you are unsure if you have the skills to accomplish it. Yet, I've discovered that these challenging experiences have been invaluable in growing my character, knowledge, and skill sets. From fixing my fridge at home to taking on business-related assignments, I'm learning to push past my perceived limitations. I discover strengths within me I may never have otherwise come across. The most important lesson learned is that we are capable of far more than what our mindsets allow us to believe. Despite difficulties or time-consuming requirements, the end-result makes it all worth it.

Each challenge has made me more confident, determined, patient, and resilient. When I was younger, my parents always told me, "If you want something, you will have to work for it" this was a source of frustration at the time because I didn't understand why they were saying this to me. Now I know it was because they wanted me to believe that there were no shortcuts, no easy way out of any situation; they wanted me to be willing to work hard for what I wanted—and they were right!

I am now much better at making decisions because of life experiences that were filled with challenges and adversities. When I had the considerable responsibility of keeping track of my younger siblings, I faced all the challenges head-on. Honestly, it had a lot to do with the way my parents included all of us in family decisions.

Today, I try my best to be an involved parent empowering my children to face their challenges. What kind of parent doesn't listen? What kind of parent doesn't care about their children? What kind of parent doesn't want their child to feel loved and cared for by their family?

That's why I advocate for involving children in family discussions at every age and stage—not just because it makes them more empathetic (which it does), but because it makes them well-rounded human beings.

After college, most people enter the workforce, a time of significant changes and new challenges. These graduates may have to move to a new city or country, learn to live on a tight budget and make new friends. Some will find jobs very different from what they expected, and others will discover that they loved college so much that they did not want to leave! Whatever the case, life after college is an exciting time full of new experiences.

In January of 1998 I transferred from Toronto, Canada, to Columbus, Ohio, to finish my last semester of college at DeVry. Two of my four younger siblings in Canada continued their education in Toronto, and the other two decided to move to New York City to complete their high school education.

## EXPLORING AND TRAVELING

After my college graduation in Columbus, my best friends, David and Hamayoun from New York, reached out with a plan for exploring the country. I was as excited about the wild adventure as they were. So instead of going back to Toronto, I went to New York. We decided to embark on a journey to visit the forty-eight continental states in the US, so we packed up a car from my hometown of New York and hit the open road. Along the way, we saw breathtaking scenery and made unforgettable memories at every destination. From majestic mountains to sweeping coastlines, we experienced it all! Despite the minor difficulties that arose due to complicated routes or inclement weather, we eventually paused our big road trip in Nashville, Tennessee, after visiting eight states. We found out that a few days staying in a hotel in Nashville was more expensive than renting a furnished apartment for a month, so we decided to rent one and visit the six remaining states surrounding Tennessee. The month flew by fast, and eventually Nashville became our new home from 1999 to 2006. That is where I found my dream job in the healthcare IT and administration field.

I chose Tennesse. The Tennessee River flows through the majestic mountains of Chattanooga, an awe-inspiring city in southeastern Tennessee. With stunning waterfalls and a 700-acre region known as "Rock City," it is no surprise that people often travel here for its rich history, rooted deep within Native American culture, or simply to take in all the natural wonders offered. But those who know better are well-aware that this legendary sight was designed by the struggles of a woman named Frieda Carter—back in 1924!

Traveling provides an unforgettable opportunity to learn and understand the hardships people have gone through in history. Get out of your comfort zone, explore new corners of the world, and discover remarkable cultures. Make sure you take advantage if you can afford it, a unique and wonderful adventure will give you valuable insights into human struggles and triumphs throughout time.

## PREPARING AND PLANNING FOR LIFE-CHANGING EVENTS

About a year after my first job, I told my family and friends that I was interested in getting married and asked if they knew someone, as I would enjoy courting the right woman. Arranged marriage in Islamic culture is an arranged introduction between a man and a woman. Other traditions of arranged marriages, where the bride and groom don't see each other until after they are pronounced husband and wife, are different. In an Islamic marriage, after the first meeting, if both parties are interested in meeting again, further dates are arranged.

My journey to get married through an arranged marriage took almost three years. I traveled from Nashville to different states in pursuit of finding my soulmate. At times, it felt like I would never find a compatible mate. I was constantly badgered and offered unsolicited advice from friends and family members. Finally, I was introduced to a friend of my mother's friend to meet her daughter while I was visiting my brother in New York. That was how I met my wife. We married on December 24, 2003.

# CHAPTER 7

# THE NECESSITY OF TRUST & MERIT

Trust keeps a relationship together; it keeps you from walking away from a situation that you have an aversion to or don't like. It is what makes you put your heart and soul into something because you know it's worth it.

We all know that trust is a vital component of any relationship. The glue that binds two people together, keeping them close and sharing their joys and sorrows. But what about merit?

Merit is the possession of skills, knowledge, qualifications, and experience that makes a person valuable in any field. Whether one applies for a job or aspires to rise through a series of promotions, great success is achieved when advancement is based solely on ability. By considering personal merit rather than outside, arbitrary factors such as race or gender, society can benefit from tapping into an individual's unique skills and abilities.

Therefore, merit-based decision-making can produce results with a far more significant impact than traditional methods. The power of merit is that it reveals each individual's best qualities and puts them in a position to share them with their community, their country, and the world.

## DEDICATION TO CONTINUOUS LEARNING

After my first business failure and upon completing my undergraduate studies, I continued my life in Nashville, where I found my first job in my field of software engineering at WebMD. The position focused on two main things. The first was fixing the Y2K issue in systems using two-digit numbers.

You may remember there was a great fear that older computers would suddenly recognize 2000 as 00 in the year date, causing computers to crash and planes to fall out of the sky. I worked on a solution for this problem to update older computers. Fortunately, my work and countless others around the country solved the problem well before it became a disaster. I also worked on updating the US healthcare system to comply with HIPAA (Health Insurance Portability and Accountability Act) of 1996 because the mandates were to start being enforced in 2002.

I initially accepted the job offer because of my passion for healthcare. However, my curiosity led me to understand US healthcare administration and the legal, functional, business, and technical aspects of the new HIPAA on my own.

I continued to advance in my career. I became an expert in healthcare administration and found financial growth opportunities based on my knowledge. As a dedicated healthcare administration professional, I am always interested in learning and staying up to date with the latest trends in the field.

Have I told you how I found my dream job within a few weeks in a strange city where I did not know anyone? I did not fear taking the first step to reach out, as I was confident in my field of study. The two most important things I did were tap into my network and distribute résumés. First, I told everyone I knew I was looking for a job and willing to relocate. Then I printed about ten résumés on fine résumé paper, walked up to the front desk of large employers, asked to speak with HR, and left them with my résumé. I received a call back from every employer!

I accepted the offer from WebMD because this job was in healthcare administration. It shows that being confident and resilient is valuable when looking for a job. Don't be afraid to take the first step and reach out to your network. You never know who can help you find your dream job.

My main goal was to save money and have a second chance to become a successful entrepreneur. I learned from my first business failure that trust is insufficient. You need a guarantor, which is often the law, which can assist when a situation gets out of control. During my first business failure, I learned that the law couldn't do much if contracts or agreements were not written. In some cases, even if in writing, the instances may be civil issues, while others may be criminal matters. Granted, that oversight in my first business venture was due to my youth and inexperience, but I vowed never to make that mistake again.

# CHAPTER 8

# IMPORTANCE OF PASSIVE INCOME

Generating passive income is the perfect way to ensure stability during uncertain times. With a bit of planning and smart investments, your financial future could flourish like never before, giving you peace of mind for whatever life throws at you next.

Before working at WebMD, I had no idea how to invest. Once I started working there and saw how much passive income some of my colleagues generated, I decided to learn about investing in the stock market, real-estate fixer uppers, and used car trades. I quickly realized that there are many ways to invest my money and that there is a lot of potential for acquiring wealth if I know what I am doing. I began investing in these three commodities, and soon I saw my assets grow.

While many invest in growing their passive income to enjoy retirement without financial worries, for me, investing in the market was not for my retirement. Instead, it was to take a second chance at establishing future business ventures.

In 1999 the NASDAQ stock market was booming, and everyone wanted to get in on the action. I decided to invest a portion of my savings and I was quickly rewarded, as the value of my shares skyrocketed. However, I knew the market was due for a correction, and I diversified my investments accordingly. As a result, although I lost a significant amount of my investment when the dot-com bubble burst, I could pull out of the market without losing everything. While it was a painful lesson, it taught me the importance of asset allocation, diversification, rebalancing my portfolio at least twice a year, and the risk-reward ratio.

However, eventually I lost trust in the stock market and turned all my investments into cash. For anyone interested in investing in the stock market, I'd say spread your risk across different asset classes. That way, if one sector crashes, you know that your other investments will help cushion the blow.

## THE SECOND START-UP

I started my second business venture by launching a chain of supermarkets. It started beautifully, having partnered with trusted friends. But good intentions and enthusiasm are not enough. It was destined to fail as none of us knew anything about the business of starting and running retail supermarkets.

It is surprising how often businesses fail because budding entrepreneurs don't take the time to develop a roadmap by developing business, marketing, and strategic plans for reaching their goals. Without a business roadmap, tracking progress, identifying obstacles, and creating contingencies to gain success can be difficult.

Surviving the first year with positive cash flow was an outstanding achievement. However, in the second year, we failed to anticipate the needs of our target market, which led to several missteps along the way. If we had taken the time to develop clear plans from the beginning, we could have saved ourselves a lot of headaches and losses totaling over $1 million.

Opening a new grocery store is no easy task and requires careful consideration. To ensure the store's success, costs must be kept low while providing customers with convenience, access, and affordability. Strategies such as effective advertising must also be employed to maximize profits. Paying attention to these factors can mean the difference between a successful business venture and one that struggles financially from the start.

The risk was huge because we all had to learn how to run supermarkets on the fly as we progressed. It was like building a plane as it was flying. The many problems proved insurmountable, and this second business also failed. The learning curve was too steep, as none of the partners had the required experience in this field.

This second business failure was far more damaging financially from a family perspective. I was newly married, and we were expecting our first child. I had to move forward with shutting down this second venture, leaving me with considerable debt.

# CHAPTER 9

# PIVOTING WITH CONFIDENCE

One of the most essential qualities for success in your personal or business life is confidence, especially when it comes to pivoting. Making a pivot means significantly changing your original plans, which can be scary. It takes a lot of confidence to pivot and even more confidence to see it through. Without confidence, you'll be second-guessing yourself at every turn.

> **It takes a lot of confidence to pivot and even more confidence to see it through.**

Your team will sense your uncertainty and will be less likely to support you. And your customers will quickly jump ship if they think you're going in the wrong direction. So, if you're contemplating pivoting, remember that confidence is vital.

## ADVANTAGE OF BEING AN EXPERT

I was able to quickly pivot based on merit; being an expert in healthcare administration and technology and having a "fall forward" attitude helped me weather the storm of this second business failure. Within two weeks, I was back on my feet, deciding to move to Washington, DC, where I would begin consulting for a federal contractor in the healthcare space and then join the second largest managed care organization, AmeriHealth Caritas, where I would work to improve healthcare information technology further.

As a healthcare management expert, I have a unique perspective on the industry. I've seen the way it works and how to improve it.

As a result, I have made significant contributions to the healthcare industry by developing better systems than are currently available. My work in converting healthcare administration into real-time administration gave healthcare providers quick access to their data in real time, which has made all the difference for patients who want to make decisions based on their health needs quickly rather than wait hours or days to receive information from their doctor's office. Worse yet, they may not receive any information because of poor communication between providers and patients.

I am driven by my desire and confidence to improve how healthcare works for everyone involved in this process: patients, providers, and administrators. My curiosity about taking a technical approach led me to win the 2009 Healthcare IT Innovation Award from Thomson Reuters.

**Indeed, not everyone who does try will become a successful entrepreneur.**

While many people may want to enter business and make a difference, as I have cited earlier, few take the plunge to start a business. Indeed, not everyone who does try will become a successful entrepreneur. I am convinced a missing component to success is knowledge.

## THIRST FOR KNOWLEDGE

Higher education is essential to business success by providing skills and knowledge that can be applied to all aspects of life, including finances, relationships with family members, friends, co-workers, and others at work or school. The skills include negotiation and conflict resolution, excellent communication, keen critical thinking, problem-solving abilities, decision-making abilities, creativity in writing or designing, financial literacy (knowing how to manage money), and computer literacy (learning how to use computers). Truly, the possibilities are endless.

Higher education can help you provide better service to your clients or customers, give you more confidence when interacting with others, and help you improve your leadership skills by acquiring various types of knowledge about leadership styles and approaches based on the uniqueness of a situation. In addition, you will develop quick thinking and manage time better to accomplish tasks faster (time management) and continually build your soft skills.

I have also learned in my business ventures that trusting my vendors and having a fallback position is often critical to guaranteeing success. The fallback position can be in the form of regulations or other laws. I also learned that I need to react very quickly on the fly and that sometimes the learning curve is very steep.

> **Whatever field you are trying to enter, it is imperative that you obtain mentors—those who know their way around the industry into which you are trying to enter.**

## SEEKING A MENTOR

Whatever field you are trying to enter, it is imperative that you obtain mentors—those who know their way around the industry into which you are trying to enter. Many companies have mentoring programs as part of their operation. If your employer has a program, take advantage of it.

If you are a business owner, learn what the S&P 500 companies have realized: mentoring is a valuable strategy, as 84 percent of US Fortune 500 companies now use mentoring programs and 100 percent of the top 50 US companies have made mentoring a go-to strategy.

You must be willing to delegate to those who know the skills you have not yet mastered. Not everyone can be a "Chief Everything Officer." No one should try to do everything themselves.

> **Not everyone can be a "Chief Everything Officer."**

A good example is Elon Musk. He started a company building electric cars and another building rockets. He did not have first-hand knowledge in either field, but he wanted to make a difference in the automotive industry and space travel, so he surrounded himself with experts in those fields.

Musk purchased Twitter for $44 billion and has made a mess by failing to appoint others more knowledgeable than himself to critical positions, which he did with Tesla and SpaceX. His first fortune was a result of co-founding PayPal. Before that, he made millions, but PayPal was his road to billions.

We could have used the advice and guidance from a few experts in grocery store management, but I am glad we attempted anyway, even though the result was a business failure. Sometimes it's enough to be audacious and take risks in a field where you have little experience because even failure brings valuable lessons.

Confidence is essential for any entrepreneur who wants to be successful. After all, starting a business is inherently risky, and it takes confidence to believe in your ideas and take the necessary risks. However, confidence alone is not enough. Entrepreneurs must also pivot confidently when their original plans don't work out. In other words, change your business model in response to feedback or

> **To be a successful entrepreneur, know that pivoting with confidence is essential.**

market conditions. It can be difficult to know when to pivot, but it is essential to have the confidence to make changes when necessary. Although making the wrong call can be costly, making the right call can lead to innovation and success. To be a successful entrepreneur, know that pivoting with confidence is essential.

# CHAPTER 10

# THE POWER OF KNOWLEDGE & EDUCATION

There is an important distinction between knowledge and education. Education is the process of acquiring systematic theoretical information. It is a formal process from a secondary school, college, trade school, or university. In contrast, knowledge is the theoretical or practical understanding of a subject. It can be acquired through education, but it can also be obtained through experience or simply by reading and studying about a subject. While education is important, it is not always necessary to have a formal education to have knowledge or subject matter expertise, which is why many say that knowledge is power and education is discipline. With knowledge, people can understand and solve new problems, even if they have not formally studied the subject.

> **Instead, I now know that knowledge is like an endless galaxy, constantly expanding and evolving.**

## KNOWLEDGE WITHOUT BOUNDARIES

As advances are made in the technological world, my opinion about knowledge is evolving. I used to believe that knowledge was like an ocean, deep and vast but with finite boundaries. Instead, I now know that knowledge is like an endless galaxy, constantly expanding and evolving. With discoveries continually being made, there is always more to learn. Just when you think you have a grasp on everything, something new comes along to challenge your understanding, which makes learning so exciting in many ways—there is always something new to explore.

There is so much to learn, and discoveries are constantly being made. We may never know everything there is to know, but the more we learn, the better we can understand ourselves and the world around us.

I have always been curious, which led me down some exciting life paths.

When I was younger, I constantly asked questions and explored the world around me. I remember spending hours in the library, poring over books about history, finance, and computers. I was fascinated by the idea of understanding how computers worked. I often checked out books about computer programming and digital design, always eager to learn more about this complex and ever-evolving field. In many ways, my love for learning has led me to where I am today. As an ambitious entrepreneur, I constantly explore new topics and seek new sources of information.

That curiosity continued into my career, where it has served me well. In my current role as the Founder and Chief Executive Officer of Eixsys, Inc. https://www.eixsys.com/, a tech company, I am responsible for computer technology research and analysis. I always look for new perspectives and try to understand the complexities of technology. It is a challenging and rewarding role, and I am grateful for the opportunity to continue learning and growing in my career.

Reflecting on my time in high school, I realized that the computer science class I took sparked my interest in computers and how they work. The course gave me a strong foundation in coding, which has helped me immensely in my career. Without that class, I might never have realized my potential in the computer science field. I was fascinated by the idea that computers could be used to solve problems, and I became interested in coding as a result. The class provided me with a basic foundation in computer science, and it sparked a lifelong interest in the subject.

After earning my high school diploma, I started

my first business venture. After my first business failure, I completed my bachelor's degree in Computer Information Systems at DeVry University. Throughout my studies, I gained valuable experience designing business automation solutions for companies in various industries. In addition, I acquired skills in multiple programming languages that proved essential in launching my career as a software engineer. Today, I am proud to say that my decision to pursue higher education has paid off in a big way. Not only have I attained a successful career, but I have also gained the knowledge and skills needed to excel in my field.

As an experienced business developer, I have taken it upon myself to impart the wisdom of my successes and failures alike to ambitious entrepreneurs. My mission is to guide them along a path toward success that avoids some of the pitfalls I encountered in my journey.

Most students at the university level struggle with figuring out what they want to do with their lives, and I was no different. I started as an accounting major, thinking I wanted to be an accountant. However, after a few weeks of study, I realized that the accounting field was not for me. So, I decided to switch my focus to computer science, and I have never looked back. The thing that I love most about computer science is that it is constantly changing. There is always something new to learn and new challenges to keep me engaged. In addition, because of the ever-changing nature of technology, my skills are always in demand.

After graduation, I started working at WebMD as a Software Engineer. There I helped in the initial phases of US Healthcare, transforming from paper-based healthcare to Electronic Data Interchange (EDI). I have always been curious, and that curiosity has served me well in my profession. When I started working in the healthcare industry, I took the time to learn as much as possible about the sector's laws and regulations.

I also immersed myself in business, learning about how healthcare organizations function and their key priorities. And, of course, I made sure to understand the job's technical aspects, such as the technicalities behind data exchange. This desire for knowledge helped me accelerate my career and allowed me to take on increasingly responsible positions. Over time, I became an expert in healthcare law; specifically the Health Insurance Portability and Accountability Act of 1996 (HIPAA), policy, and administration. That expertise has led to some amazing opportunities.

## CURIOSITY AND KNOWLEDGE

Today, I am proud to say that my curiosity has helped me build a successful career in the healthcare industry. With my computer science and healthcare systems knowledge, I am confident I will continue to succeed.

When I was younger, I was curious about finding the details about how a system or process worked. My parents used to joke, "Give it to Amin, he'll figure it out!"

After my second business failure, I returned to college for my post graduate studies. At the time, I was married and a father of two young children under four. I pursued my master's in business administration and technology management degree while my wife worked toward her master's in biomedical engineering. It was stressful, and we couldn't have done it without my mother-in-law's support.

> **Even if we lose everything else, the knowledge we have will always be with us.**

My wife and I faced the challenge of balancing family life with pursuing a master's degree. In order to make it work, she commuted between South Jersey and New York City for our first year, while I took responsibility for looking after our two young children (ages two and four). During the second year she moved in with her mother so that she could look after them both—no small feat!

It was a glorious day when we both graduated with master's degrees. Looking back, I am glad we decided to further our education. It was a tough road but worth it in the end.

Many things can be taken from us while we are alive: our money, our possessions, our health, and sometimes even our dreams, but nobody can ever take away the knowledge that we have. We can use knowledge to make better decisions, solve problems, and help others. Even if we lose everything else, the knowledge we have will always be with us. That's why knowledge is the most valuable asset that a person can possess.

## MISCONCEPTION ABOUT KNOWLEDGE

It is a common misconception that knowledge is limited to those with college degrees or white-collar jobs. Knowledge is found in all sorts of occupations, from blue-collar jobs to trade skills. Those who work with their hands have a wealth of knowledge about their craft, whether carpentry, plumbing, auto repair, or any other vocation.

This knowledge is as valuable as the theoretical knowledge gained from books and lectures. It is important to remember that there are many forms of knowledge, and each has its value. Whether someone is a doctor or a mechanic, they are both subject matter experts in their particular field.

As I was pursuing a Doctorate in Business Administration in Healthcare, I realized that my work on the dissertation in solving the healthcare interoperability issue was the springboard to my third business venture. The dissertation topic, "Healthcare interoperability, confidence, and expertise in computer science," guided me toward building my company, Eixsys, Inc. At that point I shifted my focus and energy toward this third business investment, which was the charm. It has been more successful than I ever imagined. I believe this was God's plan and will all along.

I created the business plan for Eixsys and architecture design for the interoperability solution but didn't have the time to write the software. I was looking to build an offshore software development team and was not sure where to start. I was introduced to Praful Kumar through a common friend.

Praful is an experienced and astute business leader who had recently stepped down from his role as Chief Financial Officer at Reliance Industries— India's largest private corporation. Through Praful's partnership, Eixsys, Inc was able to reach new heights in next-generation software development as he led the offshore team. His strategic insights have propelled critical financial decisions for the company to great success over the years.

# CHAPTER 11

# THE RIGHT TIMING

Have you ever had a fortuitous chance business encounter when you know that this person will be a big part of your dream coming true? Maybe you were at a networking event or sitting next to each other on a plane. Whatever the circumstances, there is something about that moment that feels right.

Business development and finding the ideal strategic partner cannot be understated. A successful partnership requires more than just an emotional connection. It requires a mutual understanding and respect for each other's strengths and weaknesses,

**Have you ever had a fortuitous chance business encounter when you know that this person will be a big part of your dream coming true?**

along with trust in their abilities to make decisions that are beneficial to both parties.

Finding the perfect fit is an art form in itself. To do this, you must think outside the box and consider qualities not traditionally associated with your ideal partner. This may include expertise, background, culture, values, and resources that add quality to your venture but are often overlooked by traditional recruitment methods.

For example, business networking meetings are vital for professionals in achieving their career goals. However, it is not always easy to find that perfect connection. It is often a matter of enviable timing and blending personalities just the right way.

There is no denying that timing plays a role in our lives. We often meet the people we are supposed to meet at precisely the right time, which is often called destiny or fate. Sometimes we take action and seize the opportunity; other times, we let it slip by because we are not ready.

So, what if you encounter the right time but don't take an action? What if you miss your chance because you are too afraid or shy, which can often happen? It doesn't mean that it was not the right time. It simply means that you were not ready for whatever reason. The key is to be open to opportunities and take action when the time is right. You never know what might happen if you do, so be ready and take a chance.

As a consumer, whether we realize it or not, we are constantly bombarded with advertising and marketing messages. The average person is now estimated to encounter 6,000 to 10,000 ads through all channels per day. Companies are always trying to sell us something, through TV commercials, sponsored posts on social media, banner advertising, billboards, magazines, newspapers, inside and outside of city business and trains, and while browsing the internet. And to be successful, they need to be persistent.

As a child, I was never sure what to do. Life was still like a puzzle: figuring out the path and trying to think through my purpose in life. As I got older, however, life began to feel less like that puzzle and more like a problem to be solved.

As I reflect on my life, I often think about that Christian nurse who cared for me after I was hit by a car. I was paralyzed for months after the accident, and my younger brother was born after a complicated delivery just days before. The nurse told my parents she would take good care of me, and she did. But the best words she ever said to me were a reminder at the right time: "God has a purpose for you in life." That beautiful message resonates with people of all faiths and has always been a source of strength for me. It was the right message at the right time.

As a teenager I went on to achieve my goals, but they weren't necessarily all that fulfilling. My childhood passion for helping the underserved faded, and instead of feeling connected to my purpose in life, I felt something was missing. I am always reminded when I listen to spiritual lectures about doing good and forbidding evil. At the time, I knew that this wasn't how it was supposed to be—that there was something more important than just getting by or reaching goals.

One day my wife was attending college, and I was walking our newborn in a stroller with my two-year-old daughter. She snapped out of my hand and ran into the street. Luckily there was no traffic, and nothing happened. But this incident triggered a memory of the magical words of the nurse who cared for me in my pain and suffering. She said, "God has a purpose for you in life." That day I vowed to take a chance at starting my own business. Faith in God was a constant reminder, and the timing was right.

I believe "God has a purpose for you in life" is true because I have known many people with similar experiences. They also have been given a chance to prove themselves. I am so grateful that I am still alive today to share my experiences with you.

Before launching my company, I designed and architected the most complex real-time data exchange system for AmeriHealth Family of

Companies, a health insurance managed-care company. It was an evolution toward not just processing real-time insurance eligibility verification, but also referrals, prior authorizations, medical alerts for gaps in care, patient medications, and many other much-needed transactions. This innovation ended nightly automated processes, which consumed costly resources. More importantly, medical decision-making happened quicker, saving many lives.

I didn't work in healthcare IT just as a job for a paycheck; I was passionate about improving the healthcare IT space. Multiple health insurance companies approached me with job offers to double my salary. However, I declined their offers because I believed the healthcare system needed significant reforms. The existing systems and processes were redundant and inefficient, often resulting in subpar patient care. I wanted to be a part of the solution.

I stopped working toward my PhD. Instead, the doctoral dissertation I had been writing became the foundation for my next business idea. I started my own company, Electronic Interoperable Exchange

Systems, now called Eixsys, Inc., to streamline healthcare IT. At Eixsys, we develop software that improves communication between doctors, patients, and hospitals.

With my confidence and expertise in computer science, I started to design business automation solutions in several industries, starting with healthcare, then jumping into other sectors, such as:

- DUI/DWI License Restoration
- E-Commerce/Supply Chain/Dropship
- Equipment Rentals
- Medical Case Management
- Security Guards Tracking and Reporting
- Real Estate MLS Data Exchange
- Towing and Scrap Metal Recycling
- Online Learning and Training
- Pharmacy Data Management
- VOIP Communication and Telemedicine
- Health and Fitness
- Salons and Reservations

- Event Scheduling and Reservations
- Food and Beverage Orders and Processing
- Political Campaign Management

That's when I learned that the power of knowledge and my passion for achieving a life mission can take me to the next level of acceleration, as this was the beginning of a very productive time in my career. I was motivated and passionate about my work as a leader in the IT innovation space.

Today companies in the public and private sectors hire my company for IT consulting and business automation system development for large and small projects. In a span of ten years, I built a team that offered innovative IT solutions in over seventeen industries with over 200 projects. My third business venture has been a great success. We have offered our customers a wide array of services and solutions, from custom software and web development to mobile application development.

I focus on dozens of work-related projects simultaneously, while maintaining responsibilities for my family, various community-based nonprofits that I serve on, neighbors, and my circle of friends. I can fulfill my responsibilities because I have my purpose of life well-defined, and I am able to prioritize.

Now that this business is off the ground, running seamlessly, and profitable, I can see it continuing to grow. However, there are so many things that I wish had done differently when I first began this journey. Now that my experience has grown, I think it is time to take another look at what went right and what can be improved.

When I started Eixsys, Inc., I was excited and energetic, eager to make it a success. But reality quickly set in, and I struggled to keep the business afloat. I was on the verge of giving up, but I decided to give it one last push and ended up finally landing a health insurance project. Thankfully, that push was enough to get the business back on track. In hindsight, I'm so grateful that I didn't give up. If I had, I would have missed the incredible satisfaction of seeing my business thrive.

The first system I developed was a healthcare interoperability solution in which medical, administrative, clinical, and medication information would flow flawlessly between disparate systems. The solution would bring the patient, provider, insurer, broker, case manager, pharmacy, and all other entities on the same page with a cost-effective approach. This Software as a Service (SaaS) solution is unique, but when I introduced the system to investors in the field, they said it would be another ten years for significant changes in healthcare laws and to adapt the system.

The delays caused a prolonged sales cycle, as it took more time for health insurers' IT departments to comprehend the solution. The first two years were rough, but I managed to keep going because of the enormous potential of my business—it was only going to get better as time went on! Unfortunately, things changed drastically after that point. My savings account ended up with a negative balance and overdraft fees. For the first time in my life, I experienced poverty. I had run out of all options. The last resort was to close the business, get a job, and borrow money.

Sometimes timing is critical to the success of a business. Farmers have long known that they can't pick a crop before it is ripe. I remember a woman appearing on one of the first episodes of Shark Tank in 2009. She sold customized, artistic surgical masks just after a minor swine flu epidemic hit the country. More than one of the Sharks noted that she was "going to need another epidemic" for her product to be successful, and at the time, 2020 was a long way off. There was no way of knowing when that next major medical emergency would happen, so none of the Sharks took up her business, which she eventually dropped and joined Google as a head of graphic arts. Presumably, she has done very well there. Unfortunately, when 2020 rolled around, she did not relaunch her business, even though the timing was then correct.

During this financial ordeal one of my best friends, Dr. Khawar Sheikh, visited me in Austin while pivoting my software development focus from healthcare to HVAC and Real-Estate property management. I had two great opportunities and commitments. First, I had to develop an Enterprise Resource Planning (ERP) solution and then offer it as "Software as a Service" (SaaS). ERP is a type of software that organizations use to manage their day-to-day business activities as a complete solution, eliminating as much human dependency to a streamlined computerized process. SaaS is a business model to offer ERP solutions in the cloud to multiple businesses in the same industry. You build it once and sell it to other companies on a monthly subscription model. Back in 2012 and 2013, it was perfect timing to build ERP solutions and offer them as SaaS in any industry.

For a small business owner, it makes perfect sense to pay a one-time setup fee and sign up for a monthly subscription instead of investing hundreds of thousands of dollars in building software and continuously maintaining it.

I told Khawar about my two initial clients and commitments in both the HVAC and real-estate industries. All I needed were the funds to invest in building the two SaaS solutions. I shared my vision to set up a nonprofit healthcare system, and an opportunity to expand Eixsys, Inc in other industries. I received the funds as a loan and hired a team consisting of a project manager, software developer, business analyst, quality assurance person, and tech lead to continue building the software.

Several months into the development of the HVAC system and ready for the first round of feedback, my client backed out. As a result, we had a fully-developed system, but no user to test. The second system for real estate was partially developed as Phase 1 but didn't move to the next phase. With the two systems halted, the funds borrowed from Khawar were lost.

In that moment I didn't know what to do. It was not just the loss of business and funds, I had a family with two young children. I also had all these products and no buyers.

It's true that God was watching my struggle and I had the power of prayer on my side. Two large clients walked through my door out of the blue and bought products I already had with services: a real-estate company and a health insurance company. This marked the takeoff stage for Eixsys, Inc.

Once again, I learned to never underestimate the power of prayer. After this, we created SaaS solutions for many other companies, landed multiple projects, and everything changed. Although extremely hectic, it was the right time to have developed ERP solutions and offer them as SaaS. I thank God that things worked out for the better.

After positively impacting multiple industries, I joined the most innovative and progressive chamber in the Central Texas region, The Round Rock Chamber of Commerce. I enrolled in the Ambassador Program as a volunteer and was appointed as a board member, supporting economic development in the region. It is vital for an economic chamber to hire the right staff to understand the Chamber's needs and guide members through their journey. I was blessed to have met the Chamber's Investor Development Director, Laura McManus, in my early journey as part of the Chamber, where I learned about many opportunities and ensured I did not miss any meetings.

Through the Chamber events, I was fortunate to meet Zahir Walji, a brilliant mind in business. He brought a unique perspective of an idea that brings forth a challenge you might experience later down the road. When I launched a networking group for business owners only (Mars Networking), I suggested he attend a few sessions and provide feedback. Zahir gave a detailed breakdown on issues such as defining purpose and listing rules for the group. Through the years, Zahir has provided me with guidance on many occasions.

Success is a path with challenges and does not happen overnight. As new projects from multiple companies rolled in, a legal challenge came along as well.

> **Success is a path with challenges and does not happen overnight.**

In the US, anyone can sue anyone for anything, but the burden of proof falls on the plaintiff. Managing multiple new projects while going through the legal battle was brutal. I was sued for over half a million dollars and accused of nineteen frivolous claims.

After consulting with my friend, Jim Howicz, JD, a great business attorney and managing partner of one of the largest law firms in Austin, Texas, I decided to fight the case. Jim is not a litigation attorney, but he reviewed everything and suggested we fight the case to win. If I settle, then I agree with all false accusations. But if I fight, I can win and clear my name of all nineteen counts of the plaintiff's charges. Jim said I had a strong case. I told him I needed a female lawyer, as I have a house full of women. I was a husband and a father of two young daughters at the time and admired their strength in remembering details. Jim recommended Anna Eby.

The legal discovery phase started; the plaintiff's lawyer sent ambiguous requests causing my attorney to file objections that led to putting motions in court and then attending court for hearings. This process lasted for almost two years. Finally, right outside the courtroom door and right before the jury trial began, the plaintiff and his attorney offered to settle.

I refused their offer, and we started on the week-long trial. Anna Eby remembered every detail, many of which I had forgotten. She remembered every text and email message between the plaintiff and me. She remembered hours and hours of lengthy depositions. Finally, the jury announced their verdict. They unanimously declared me as "Not Guilty," and the plaintiff "Guilty" of fraud in the counter lawsuit filed against the plaintiff, a cardiothoracic surgeon. He breached a non-disclosure agreement and intentionally hid a conflict of interest that led to a breach of the contractual obligation.

During this two-year legal battle, I lost many new clients, as I could not commit my time to business development. I went through a long period of Discovery, the formal process of exchanging information between the parties about the witnesses and evidence each side will present at trial. I was called in for deposition after deposition, going to the court for multiple hearings on motions filed by the plaintiff, going through mediation and finally, a week-long jury trial.

What do "Give First" and "Forgive First" mean? What I learned in life and described in the chapter,

**Move On—Stop Living in the Past,** helped me to put the needs of others ahead of my own, and I am quick to forgive when someone does something to hurt or upset me. I think this approach to life has served me well, both in personal relationships and business dealings.

I believe that my willingness to "Give First" and "Forgive First" allowed me to avoid another legal battle with another group of business owners who violated their contracts. We had a written agreement stipulating that any partner who left the joint venture would have to pay a penalty of $1 million. But instead, I chose to forgive them and focus on the future. This decision helped me avoid a lengthy and costly legal battle.

> **Do not sign a contract if you cannot fulfill the contractual obligation.**

Joint ventures are beneficial for two or more entities, but at the same time very risky if one entity does not fulfill its role and obligation. Each entity must understand the effort it takes to build a joint venture and the financial consequences on the other entities leaving in the middle of an agreement. If I had left the joint venture in the middle of the formation, I know for sure two companies would have claimed bankruptcy, and legally I would owe each of them $1 million.

My advice is to always sign a contract. It is better to have something in writing presented in the court rather than arguing "he said" or "she said." Additionally, do not sign a contract if you cannot fulfill the contractual obligation. Always write an email or text that can be presented in court like all my emails and texts were during my trial.

If you ever struggle with a business venture, remember that it is never too late to turn things around. Also, it is true: running a business is not everyone's forté. However, with a little effort and determination, you can achieve anything you want. Take risks! If you are waiting on your couch for the **right time** or opportunity, it won't arrive. You must proactively go out and do something!

We all have regrets in life. Whether it is a relationship we didn't pursue, a job we turned down, or a chance we didn't take, regrets can weigh heavily on our hearts and minds. However, it is important to remember that most regrets are acts of omission. We often regret what we didn't try rather than what we did because we naturally focus on the what-ifs and could-haves rather than the reality of the

**Take risks! If you are waiting on your couch for the right time or opportunity, it won't arrive.**

situation. If only we had taken that job, if only we had attended that meeting, if only we had gone on that trip—the list goes on and on. But dwelling on these could-haves is a recipe for a life of regrets. I didn't want to say what-if or could-have as a regret for not trying that option. Instead, I took it one step further by taking on another risk.

# CHAPTER 12

# BUILDING A LEGACY THROUGH MISSION-DRIVEN GIVING

In today's society, getting lost in the rat race of working long hours to make ends meet is easy. Unfortunately, we overlook the capabilities, qualities, and opportunities people around us do not have. As a result, finding the time and volunteering to pursue our instinct to help others becomes difficult.

Anyone can make a difference by giving back, whether it is through time, donations, or simply listening. But those who want to create a lasting legacy usually focus on one issue or specific group of people, which allows them to dive deep into knowing the issue they are helping and understanding the community's needs. Legacy-building isn't about sporadic acts of kindness; it is about finding a cause you're passionate about and making a lifelong commitment to it. And that's something that anyone can do.

However, it is important to remember that the value is not in completing your mission but in being persistent. When you are clear about your goals and committed to your path, you will continue to move forward even when faced with setbacks.

> **Legacy-building isn't about sporadic acts of kindness; it is about finding a cause you're passionate about and making a lifelong commitment to it.**

When you first commit to living your life with a mission to give back to others, you hope the lives you touch will eventually touch many other lives. It's called *paying it forward.* You want to make a difference in the world, and you know that even if you can't change everything, you can at least positively impact those around you.

You may not see the results of your efforts immediately, but over time you hope your example will inspire others to do the same. It is about planting the seeds of kindness and compassion and then trusting that they will grow and blossom in their own time. Of course, it is not always easy to stay the course. But if you keep your eyes on the prize and remind yourself why you are doing this in the first place, you can persevere through any challenge.

After my accident, I was tended to by a nurse who went above and beyond her call of duty. Not only did she stay with me after her shift ended, but she also came in early the next morning to make sure I was comfortable. Her selfless acts of kindness left a lasting impression on me, and I have always sought to give back similarly.

Whether volunteering at a local soup kitchen or donating clothes to a shelter, I always try to help those in need. I know that I would not be where I am today without the kindness of others, and I am committed to paying it forward. Giving back is a rewarding experience. With so much negativity in the world, acts of kindness can make a real difference.

Our sincere faith in God reminds us of being selfless, and when we are selfless, we act out of concern for the well-being of others without any regard for ourselves. As humans, we tend to have egocentric traits. However, as we grow older, most of us become more aware of the world around us, and we realize there are underserved people in our lives who have needs and feelings,

**If you keep your eyes on the prize and remind yourself why you are doing this in the first place, you can persevere through any challenge.**

too. We learn that we can make a difference in the lives of others by giving selflessly of our time, energy, and resources. When we give selflessly, we improve the lives of those we serve while enriching our own.

There are many ways to give selflessly. You can volunteer your time to help those in need, donate money or goods to charitable organizations, or perform acts of kindness for others. No matter how you choose to give, selfless giving is always appreciated and makes a difference in this world.

From a young age, I was incredibly touched by the selfless acts of my medical providers. They helped save my life and inspired me to live life to the fullest. As a result, I always wanted to create something that would make a difference in the world.

# CHAPTER 13

# VISION AND MISSION-DRIVEN ORGANIZATION

After my third startup's success, I wanted to do more than write a check for a charity. I wanted to create something that would have an immediate and lasting impact, so I ended up starting a nonprofit that would focus on healthcare. The initial goal was to create a hospital, but the nonprofit became a community health center establishing primary and preventative healthcare clinics for the uninsured and underinsured.

This organization is a platform for volunteer medical providers to work together to provide life-saving care to those in need. In addition to providing primary health care, we also work to raise awareness about the importance of preventative healthcare.

Life can be hectic, and it is easy to get caught up in your day-to-day life. As a result, you often don't have time to think about others and how you can help them. However, it is essential to remember that you can make a difference in the lives of those around you.

As Dr. Martin Luther King, Jr. famously said, "Life's most persistent and urgent question is, 'What are you doing for others?'" I was determined never to have that question posed to me because I wanted the answer to be obvious to everyone. Everyone can do something to make the world a better place, no matter how big or small the gesture may be. If I can do it from my humble beginnings, so can you.

Inspired by medical providers, the nonprofit healthcare I founded was named Eixsys Healthcare

System (EHS) https://www.ehsclinic.org/; it was named after my third business venture: Eixsys.

Today EHS is expanding medical clinic locations in communities it believes will make a real difference in people's lives. EHS works closely with those communities to ensure their resources are effectively used.

Like a stone thrown into a pond, the good done by our nonprofit will create ever-expanding ripples of positive change. Already, we see this in our communities, and I am confident that this will continue to grow in the months and years to come.

When I established EHS as a technology professional, I envisioned creating a healthcare system that would be easy for any community center to replicate and start a volunteer-run medical clinic. Instead, through this healthcare nonprofit, we have established several charity clinics that serve the underserved and uninsured in the communities in which they were established. As a result, we have helped countless individuals receive the medical care they need and deserve.

Certainly, starting any organization comes with challenges; this is especially true for tax-exempt nonprofits, which rely heavily on volunteers and donations. When everyone has a say in what happens, and no one wants to take full responsibility for an action, it can lead to more challenges because volunteers can be difficult to hold accountable if they don't show up when needed. While nonprofit organizations do important work in our communities, they must overcome these challenges to succeed.

After launching the EHS project, I was working on marketing my project when I met Cristal Finke through a mutual friend. I immediately noticed her kind nature and willingness to help others. So, I asked Cristal if she would help and support this nonprofit effort. She took the responsibility to set up the first clinic and as many subsequent clinics as needed, entirely through volunteering.

Additionally, she used her car to transport people and materials to ensure the project would succeed. Special thanks go to her parents, Dennis and Helen Finke, for supporting and encouraging

Cristal to continue with selfless acts of charity.

The second and third most significant people I met who helped make the clinics a reality were Imam Islam Mossaad and Sunita Murti. In 2006 on my first attempt to move to Austin, Texas, I met Imam Islam Mossaad, the spiritual leader of North Austin Muslim Community Center. In 2010 when I returned to Austin to register my tech company, I met Sunita Murti, one of the founders and Trustees of Austin Hindu Temple and Sai Baba Temple in Cedar Park, Texas.

I shared my vision with them for a nonprofit healthcare organization, and without any hesitation, they both volunteered to help in any capacity they could. Through Sunita Murti's support, we launched our clinic at the Austin Hindu Temple, and through the support of Imam Islam Mossaad, we launched our clinic at North Austin Muslim Community Center in 2015.

In its second year of operation, the clinic received a notice from its medical director to immediately remove her name from all records and cease

any association with the clinic. There was no expla-
nation other than the warning of legal action if
orders were not followed. The clinic was without a
medical director for two weeks. I was worried we'd
have to shut down the clinic.

Then, after one Friday prayer, Dr. Faris Hashim,
a pediatric nephrologist, approached me because
someone had told him about the charity clinic. Dr.
Faris had relocated to Austin from Florida and was
interested in volunteering his time. I had the opportunity to explain to him why EHS exists and that we
were in dire need of a medical director. He immediately agreed to help. His wife, Manal, a licensed
medical assistant, also joined us as a volunteer. As
a result of their willingness to help, the free clinic
stayed open and continues serving the underserved
in Austin.

We were joined by Dr. Tarik Malick and his
wife, Dr. Sadia Rashid, who were raising their toddler
and an infant while working full time. They decided
to volunteer their time and give back to the community. Dr. Kiran Chaudhry stepped up even after the

death of her husband while raising her son as a single mother and working full time. Dr. Marrium Mouti joined while working full time, doing her fellowship in neurology, and raising two sons. Dr. Madhu Huda and Dr. Sukanya Burugu joined as they worked full time, raising their children and caring for their parents. Dr. Durreshawar Khan proposed she would go out to the homeless shelters and treat patients there, and this journey continued as hundreds of physicians joined and continued to join and give back.

Physicians and faith-based community centers are joining to provide volunteer-based medical clinics and replicate the EHS model.

**If you can stay resilient, others will likely follow your lead. After all, people are drawn to those who know what they are doing.**

Anyone who has started a new project knows there is always an adjustment period. There will inevitably be challenges, whether you are embarking on a new business venture, starting a family, or simply trying to establish a new habit. However, the key to success is persevering through these tough times and never giving up on your dreams. If you can stay resilient, others will likely follow your lead. After all, people are drawn to those who know what they are doing. So, if you want to achieve something great, don't be afraid of a little struggle—it is an integral part of the journey.

# CHAPTER 14

# BECOMING A SERVANT LEADER

Servant leadership is a term that Robert K. Greenleaf first coined in *The Servant as Leader*, an essay he published in 1970. In his essay, Greenleaf argues that the only way to truly lead is by serving others, which means putting the needs of others above your own and acting to benefit them, not yourself. While it may seem counterintuitive, servant leaders are often some of the most successful leaders because they can build trust and inspire loyalty. They create a positive work environment where everyone can thrive. Servant leadership is a great option.

Moving through the world with the intention of *Give First and Take Last* can feel counterintuitive. We have been taught since birth to put ourselves first, to look out for our interests, and to take what we can while the taking is good. But what if we could act from a place of selflessness and compassion instead? When we give first, we open the possibility for others to do the same.

**A person who constantly focuses on taking and not giving gets into a vicious cycle of deprivation, feeling as if society has taken away his rights.**

A person who constantly focuses on taking and not giving gets into a vicious cycle of deprivation, feeling as if society has taken away his rights. Acting in destructive ways is seen as the only way to get it back. This mindset multiplies and destroys communities by stealing their full potential of achieving through the path of struggle.

All of us are born with a fundamental desire to belong and to be cared for. As seen in gang activities, young people from disadvantaged backgrounds join together to get the money, power, and respect they think they have been denied. When people feel their basic needs have not been met, they may resort to extreme measures to get what they believe is rightfully theirs.

## LEADERSHIP

In 2016 I was selected to participate in the Leadership Round Rock class, an incredible honor and opportunity to learn more about the civic engagement process and local leadership from some of the most respected names in the field. I was particularly inspired by Andy Webb and Ryan McGahey, who chaired and co-chaired the leadership class. Under their guidance, I learned much about what it takes to be an effective leader. I also had the chance to observe firsthand the dedication and commitment our elected officials have in making Round Rock a better place.

Additionally, I was fortunate to receive leadership advice and mentorship from Round Rock City Council Member, Will Peckham, and Round Rock Chamber Chair-Elect, Lora Weber. Will and Lora are tremendous leaders in their own right and their insights and guidance have been invaluable, as I continue my journey as a leader in the Round Rock community.

I have always been interested in civic leadership and the role of government in improving our world. However, after getting involved I had the opportunity to see this work from a new perspective. I met many city, county, state, and federal officials and learned firsthand about their work. I was impressed by their dedication to public service and commitment to making a difference. I also saw the practical side of servant leadership. These officials are often called upon to help those in need, and they do so with compassion and care.

I am grateful for the opportunity to see civic

leadership from this new perspective, and I am convinced that it is essential work that positively impacts our world.

The Williamson County public officials I met and their passion for serving the emerging diverse community were mind-boggling. I learned that these elected officials care for and are passionate about their city, county, and state's future, economy, infrastructure, healthcare, and everything else.

Their passion makes them great leaders. All of them have dedicated many years to ensuring our city had what it needed to attract businesses, families, and visitors. The elected officials worked tirelessly to improve resources for their constituents while keeping taxes low. Thanks to their efforts and everyone serving before them, Williamson County is emerging as a destination county for many young families. We are fortunate to have such dedicated leaders represent us over the years.

Williamson County is rapidly growing in the central Texas metropolitan area. The county has recently experienced an influx of new residents and businesses. While this growth has brought many benefits to the community, it has also put a strain on local infrastructure and services. Fortunately, the county has benefited from strong leadership at the local level. County officials have worked tirelessly to ensure that all cities and municipalities remain safe and welcoming places for all.

As a result of their efforts, Williamson County has maintained its small-town feel even as it continues to grow. This leadership has made a big difference in county residents' quality of life and has helped set it apart from its neighboring counties.

The Leadership Round Rock class inspired me to adopt servant leadership qualities in my work at the nonprofit healthcare organization Eixsys Healthcare System. I observed how they always put the needs of others before their own and efficiently resolved any issues that arose, which made me realize that effective leaders do not need to micromanage; instead, they should focus on enabling those they lead to reach their full potential.

I applied this new perspective in my role at Eixsys and found that it helped to create a more positive and productive work environment. As a result, I am now a strong advocate for servant leadership and its ability to create lasting change.

Resilience is a quality we all need to adopt in order to achieve our goals and build a better future for ourselves and our community. It is the ability to bounce back from setbacks, learn from our mistakes, and keep moving forward despite tough situations. Resilience allows us to pick ourselves up after a fall and keep going. It helps us find the strength to face each new day. And it enables us to build a better future for ourselves and those around us. So never give up, never give in, and always keep striving toward your goals. Having resilience and an excellent quality of servant leaders is the key to success; they push themselves to achieve new heights and encourage others.

I believe seeking and serving in public office can make a person more sensitive to the need to become a servant of the community. It is necessary for those in politics to orient their attitude in this direction because they will frequently be asked to make decisions and take up legislation that will affect hundreds of thousands, if not millions, of people.

Pause for a minute and think of the leaders around you: a mother taking responsibility for nourishing her baby, a father looking out for and protecting his family, a religious leader leading the community congregation, a project leader, or an organization leader improving the work environment. They are all leaders.

When you focus on the well-being of others, there is a positive rippling effect that benefits everyone. When you are honest and have integrity, others trust you and feel confident following your lead. They are attracted to your positive qualities: selfless, humble, and focused on the collective good. These are essential for any leader who wants to build a thriving community.

CHAPTER 15

# BUILDING ALLIANCES IS BUILDING A COMMUNITY AT LARGE

A community at large is like a family of various smaller communities; it is a group of individuals with different backgrounds, beliefs, and experiences who come together to support and care for one another. When a community is united on common ground, it can flourish. Common ground gives community members a sense of belonging and creates a shared identity. It also allows community members to work together toward common goals. In contrast, when a community is divided on differences, members are more likely to view each other with suspicion and mistrust, which leads to conflict and division rather than cooperation and unity.

> **When a community is united on common ground, it can flourish.**

In my community, there is a lot of focus on politics. People often get caught up in supporting a particular party or candidate without thinking about the issues that matter most to the community. I have always believed that we should focus on solving common problems. I think this is especially important when it comes to community involvement. We can make a real difference in our community by coming together and working toward solving the issues that matter most to us. This philosophy has served me well in my community involvement, and I believe it can help us make positive and sustaining changes.

Anyone who is paying attention to current events knows that there are a lot of issues that need to be solved. And it often seems like people would rather talk about them instead of taking action to solve them. One issue that I am particularly passionate about is access to healthcare. It has been over ten years since I started the Eixsys Healthcare System (EHS) project, which has now morphed into a nonprofit healthcare organization dedicated to improving healthcare access.

When we started, we had just one charity clinic that served those who fell through the cracks and couldn't afford healthcare. In this case, we took a private sector and community approach to solving this problem instead of becoming a burden on taxpayers. We have come a long way in the past ten years, but more work still needs to be done. I will not stop fighting until everyone has the same opportunity to receive quality medical care, no matter where they live or how much money they have.

I am often asked why I share my time, knowledge, talents, and resources with others. And what do I hope to gain from it? The answer is simple: my actions are louder than my words, and I am expressing my gratitude for the opportunity of life given by God. I don't just want to reap the benefits of the hard work our predecessors have done, but rather contribute my efforts toward improving and building a community.

As mentioned in the Quran (2:254) "O you who believe! Spend out of what We have provided you before there comes a Day when there will be no buying and selling..."

> My actions are louder than my words, and I am expressing my gratitude for the opportunity of life given by God.

I have been fortunate enough to have been given a great deal in life; a loving family, a good education, and many opportunities.

As a result, I feel a responsibility to give back to those who are less fortunate. By volunteering my time and resources, I can help make a difference in the lives of others. And that is truly rewarding. Seeing the smiles on their faces after I've helped them makes me feel like I've made the world just a little bit better.

> **We live in a world where we are constantly taking and seldom giving. We can all benefit from turning this paradigm on its head and choosing to give first.**

We live in a world where we are constantly taking and seldom giving. We can all benefit from turning this paradigm on its head and choosing to give first. When we give of ourselves, we open up the possibility of receiving so much more in return. We create connections and build relationships. We make a difference in the lives of others. Next time you are tempted to ask, "What's in it for me?" try to give and see what you receive in return.

Giving first has always been an essential part of who I am. Whether extending a helping hand to someone in need or being the first to offer kindness, I believe we all can make a difference in the world. In societies where so much focus is placed on individual achievement, don't forget that it is more important than ever to give back. We all have the power to make a difference.

While financial giving is important, it is not the only way to give. You can give your time, but one of the most valuable things you can provide are connections. Connecting people to other resourceful individuals can make a real difference in someone's life. And that's the true spirit of giving.

In any given society, there are problems. It is essential to be clear that some of these problems may not have easy solutions. Differences will always exist among people, leading to misunderstanding and possible conflict.

However, finding ways to resolve these differences and reach a mutually acceptable agreement is possible. In some cases, this may require compromise on both sides. That being said, it is important to note that conflict is not always bad. On the contrary, it can lead to positive change and growth in a society if the two sides choose to work together and not give up until a solution has been reached.

# CHAPTER 16

# FINAL THOUGHTS

Give First and Take Last changes the perspective of how you view the world. You don't necessarily have to face life-threatening injuries as a child, like I did, to adopt this perspective. Everyone will have different turning points they can look back on and say to themselves. *This was the reason I decided to change the direction of my life.*

My experiences, even difficult ones like repeatedly failing in business ventures, can create positive outcomes that teach valuable lessons and build resilience and character within us. Even the most traumatic experience can lead to positive lessons we can learn.

That is an important message to take away from this book. **Failure is never final, and lessons can be learned from the worst failures.** Life is a series of adventures; sometimes, those adventures fail. But **failure is something that builds resilience in you** if you allow it to. You must first decide that failure is not final and is simply part of life and exists for you to build resilience and learn positive lessons.

There is a famous saying that goes like this: "It's always darkest before the dawn," and Dr. Martin Luther King, Jr. once said something similar, "But I know, somehow, that only when it is dark enough can you see the stars."

Even during failure there are glimmers of hope. And looking back on failures, as I have done throughout this book, it is often easy to see valuable lessons that can be learned from those mistakes.

The famous motivational author, Napoleon Hill once said, "Every failure brings with it the seed of an equivalent success." That is a great insight and it is true. The author Bruce Van Horn says, "Every experience is your teacher; everything is for your growth."

Through my interactions with all the people I have encountered, from family to friends and beyond, I am genuinely thankful for each lesson they've imparted. But, of course, my wife stands out among these relationships, as she's been a source of stability in times when things seemed unpredictable, driving me toward creating something meaningful while ensuring that if ever needed, there is someone who will pick me up again.

If building a legacy is your ultimate goal, then building resilience becomes a necessity. It is like the farmer or the car mechanic who builds up calluses on their hands from hard work. Those calluses are symbols of the resilience that they gain from the hard work they perform.

Giving First or extending a hand of gratitude toward other communities dissolves the hostility between

> **If building a legacy is your ultimate goal, then building resilience becomes a necessity.**

individuals and those communities. By approaching life as a way to give back, by giving first and expecting no return, we build goodwill and friendships and send out "good vibes."

That is the challenge I wish to leave you with: go out into your community and do good. Give First, even before someone asks you for help.

And whatever you do, don't ever get discouraged by failures when they do happen. The investor and business consultant Sahil Bloom once wrote, "Ships don't sink because of the water around them; ships sink because of the water that gets in them. So don't let what's happening around you get inside you and weigh you down."

Made in the USA
Middletown, DE
12 July 2024